Imperial Dominion
and
Priestly Genius

Imperial Dominion

and

Priestly Genius

Coercion, Accommodation, and Resistance in the Divorce Rhetoric of Ezra-Nehemiah

Herbert Robinson Marbury

Sopher Press
Upland, California

TABLE OF CONTENTS

Preface

This book began as a research project long put away as I embarked upon what I believed at the time to be more worthy academic pursuits. Then, in 2005, my graduate seminar "Empire and Canon," investigating the evidence for assigning portions of the Hebrew Bible to Persian period Jerusalem, reminded me of the connection between my current interests in the politics of discursive production of the politics of the divorce rhetoric in Ezra-Nehemiah (Ez. 9-10 and Neh. 10, 13). According to this study's thesis, the Second Temple priesthood of Persian Jerusalem constructed that divorce rhetoric as a deliberately polyvalent discourse to articulate vastly different messages to the imperial authorities on the one hand and to the Second Temple community on the other. At political, cultic, and economic levels, the rhetoric's meanings participated in affirming both Persian dominion and counterhistorical resistance.

The study bears the imprint of my own deep commitments to historical-critical and hermeneutical methods. My interest here is not in doing "new history" but in demonstrating connections between a historical world and that world's rhetorical politics, and so I ground the rhetoric in the particular world shaped by the politics of Persian dominion. I show how the divorce rhetoric of Ezra-Nehemiah forms counter-narratives of resistance for literate elites as they maintain the religious and cultural integrity of the Second Temple community. The last section of each of the three—political, cultic, and economic—critiques takes a Gadamerian turn by interpreting meaning for within the rhetoric political world, but brackets "true-ness" (*Wahrheit*) until the critique completes a thorough historical investigation.

The study has also benefitted from the insights of my former teachers and colleagues at Vanderbilt University. My research continues to owe much to Renita J. Weems for her guidance as a skilled adviser long ago when I was a student. Douglas A. Knight read and offered important critiques on entire drafts. Both Annalisa Azzoni and Jack M. Sasson read chapters and lent their vast expertise in all matters Ancient Near East (ANE). Alice W. Hunt has been a worthy interlocutor. Outside of Hebrew Bible, Victor Anderson and Lewis V. Baldwin offered insightful questions and rigorous critique, and pressed me to grasp the project's relevance beyond my discipline. Dale Andrews, Forrest Harris, Stacey M. Floyd-Thomas, and Juan M. Floyd-Thomas have left nothing wanting as supportive colleagues. Beyond Vanderbilt, I have benefitted from robust and generative conversations with a wider community of biblical scholars, namely Charles B. Copher, Randall C. Bailey, Michael J. Brown, Monya A. Stubbs, and Love Sechrest. Much of this work was vetted in the Social Scientific Criticism of the Second Temple Period group at successive meetings of the Society of Biblical Literature. Bailey, Copher, and Brown gave generously of their time and insight. I am particularly grateful to John Halligan, Melody Knowles, and Philip Davies for their insightful critiques. Jason Michael Smith sleuthed footnotes and Christopher T. Paris graciously did last minute copyediting. Ulrike Guthrie lent her superior editing skills. I am greatly indebted to Jon L. Berquist for years of Yehud conversations and professional encouragement. Early on, Jon recognized value in this study and encouraged it toward publication.

I am most grateful to my family. Andrew and Sheryl opened their home and offered me a place to write, to think, and to be. Antonio Meeks offered constant presence and unwavering support. My nephews, Lawrence and Jaylen, ensured that I put my pen down to go to the movies, while my niece, Chloe, brought me smiles. My grandmother, Ernestine Robinson, equipped me with diligence by requiring me to do my homework over again and again despite my protests. Lastly, I am grateful to my parents, Herbert L. and Annette R. Marbury, who taught me to think critically about the world around me.

List of Abbreviations

AJSL	*American Journal of Semitic Languages and Literature*
ABD	*Anchor Bible Dictionary.* Edited by D. N. Freedman. 6 vols. New York: Doubleday, 1992
AEL	Ancient Egyptian Literature. M. Lichtheim. 3 vols. Berkeley: University of California Press, 1971-1980.
AoF	Altorientalische Forschungen
AOS	American Oriental Series
CAH	Cambridge Ancient History
CHJ	*Cambridge History of Judaism.* Edited by W. D. Davies and Louis Finkelstein. Cambridge: Cambridge University Press, 1984–
COS	*The Context of Scripture.* Edited by W. W. Hallo. 3 vols. Leiden: Brill, 1997—2002.
FCB	Feminist Companion to the Bible
JBL	*Journal of Biblical Literature*
JCS	*Journal of Cuneiform Studies*
JNES	*Journal of Near Eastern Studies*
JSOTSup	Journal for the Study of the Old Testament Supplement Series
JSS	*Journal of Semitic Studies*
RHR	*Revue de l'histoire des religions*
SBLDS	Society of Biblical Literature Dissertation Series
SBLMS	Society of Biblical Literature Monograph Series
SBLSymS	Society of Biblical Literature Symposium Series
Sem	*Semeia*
VT	*Vetus Testamentum*
VTSup	Vetus Testamentum Supplements
ZAW	*Zeitschrift für die alttestamentlich Wissenschaft*

Chapter 1

Introduction

Persian Period: A Dismal Age No More

    The Persian period has long been the neglected stepchild of biblical scholarship. As early as the late nineteenth century, Julius Wellhausen characterized the era as a dark age in the history of ancient Israel. Following Wellhausen's turn to the Golden Age of the Israelite monarchy and the world of the prophets to recover "authentic" Israelite religion, studies through the better portion of the twentieth century preferred to focus on earlier eras of ancient Israel's story. Many of those studies focused on the Deuteronomistic Historian's retrospective accounts of the era of the Davidic monarchy, such as the romanticized stories of triumph, tragedy, and intrigue composed about David, the musician, lover, and warrior king; the idealized wisdom of King Solomon, the temple builder; and the fascinating villainy of Jezebel and Ahab. Other studies turned to the classical prophets, focusing on the heroic portrayals of figures such as Jeremiah and Amos, their insistent calls for justice, or their rhetoric's colorful vitriol.

    Despite the comparative lack of attention given to it, the Persian period is not a dismal age in the history of ancient Israel; rather, as scholars date more texts to the period of Persian domination, it has become understood as an era of tremendous formational significance for the Yahwistic community in Jerusalem, and particularly as the period from which much of the literature of the Hebrew Bible began to emerge. Instead of being the stepchild of biblical scholarship, the Persian period is now the golden child. Philip Davies argues,

> This latter society [that is 'biblical Israel'] is born only
> in the Persian period, and in that sense the biblical
> literature, as opposed to relics which it incorporated and
> re-formed and re-contextualized, is a product of what we
> call the Second Temple Period...[1][and]... the formation
> of a corpus of literature which comes to be the Bible
> starts within the society created in Judah in the Persian
> period.[2]

If Davies's conclusions are correct, then Persian period study is properly
the study of the literary history of the monarchy and the prophets. The
stories of the matriarchs, patriarchs, prophets, and monarchy took their
final form in the framework of Persian imperial dominion.

In the decades since Davies's 1992 claim, more scholars have
understood the Persian Period as a generative era for ancient Israel's
literature. In fact, scholarly perspectives on the Persian period changed
dramatically throughout the latter part of the twentieth century. Whereas
formerly scholars claimed that the Persian period was a dismal era in the
history of ancient Israel, an era in which priestly legalism held captive
the natural religion of Yahwism,[3] more recently the Persian period has
become the subject of new arguments based on social scientific
methodologies[4] that allow scholars to surmise different groups and how

---

[1] Philip R. Davies, *In Search of 'Ancient Israel'* (JSOTSup148; Sheffield:
Sheffield Academic Press, 1992), 91.

[2] Davies, *In Search of*, 95.

[3] See, for example, Douglas A. Knight, "Wellhausen and the Interpretation of
Israel's Literature," *Semeia* 25 (1982): 21-36.

[4] For example, see Daniel L. Smith, *The Religion of the Landless : A Social
Context of the Babylonian Exile* (Bloomington, Ind.: Meyer-Stone Books, 1989).
Smith turns to insights from anthropology to argue that the rhetoric in Ezra-
Nehemiah reflected the postexilic community's need for religious and ethnic
identity maintenance. Kenneth Hoglund's description of Yehudite society uses
archaeological data and Shmuel Noah Eisenstadt's structural-functional theory
of the political systems of empires. See S. N. Eisenstadt, *The Political Systems
of Empires: The Rise and Fall of Historical Bureaucratic Societies* (New York:
Free Press, 1969). Kenneth Hoglund, *Achaemenid Administration in Syria-*

they may have functioned in Yehudite society. These new arguments also allow us to conjecture a more detailed picture of the social matrix of Yehud.

Still, more accurate descriptions of Yehud notwithstanding, beginning with Wellhausen, scholarly reconstructions of Yehudite society have become more divergent. Consequently, our concept of the nature of the relationship of the political, economic, and religious groups and forces that shaped Persian Yehud remains unresolved. The current state of scholarship leaves several questions unanswered: What groups constituted the province of Yehud and specifically, the city of Jerusalem? What webs of relations existed between them? How was power shared or distributed among them? How did these groups find social and political legitimation? What were their authority structures? One way of disclosing the nature of the groups and forces that shaped Yehud is by studying the rhetoric they produced.

Rhetoric, Politics, and Polyvalence

Rhetoric is discourse that intends to induce the cooperation of the hearer,[5] and as such it is inextricably connected to the social world. Rhetoric performs everyday common social activities such as establishing friendships, signifying enemies, negotiating with kinspeople to whom one belongs, pursuing self-interests, and creating a view of the world that offers a sense of security and a vision of greater things to be

---

Palestine and the Missions of Ezra and Nehemiah (Atlanta: Scholars Press, 1992), 92-96. See also Jon L. Berquist, *Judaism in Persia's Shadow: A Social and Historical Approach* (Minneapolis: Fortress, 1995), 241-55. Berquist discusses the efficacy and the limitations of using a social and historical approach to reconstruct Yehudite society. He extensively uses Eisenstadt's theories to reconstruct the politics of the Persian Empire. Most recently, Charles E. Carter has used archaeological and anthropological approaches to depict Persian Yehud (*The Emergence of Yehud in the Persian Period: A Social and Demographic Study* [Sheffield: Sheffield Academic Press], 1999).

[5] Bernard L. Brock, Robert L. Scott, and James W. Chesebro, "An Introduction to Rhetorical Criticism," in *Methods of Rhetorical Criticism: A Twentieth-Century Perspective* (ed. Bernard L. Brock, Robert L. Scott, and James W. Chesebro; Detroit: Wayne State University Press, 1990), 9–23.

achieved both in this life and after it.[6] At the heart of social conflicts, the privileged, the powerful, and the literate deploy rhetoric to shape opinion, to frame social phenomena, to persuade the masses, and to direct power to achieve particular ends. This study argues that the divorce rhetoric of Ezra-Nehemiah (Ezra 9-10 and Neh 10, 13) condemning marriage outside the community and indeed country, is one such example. With mass divorces as its subject, the rhetoric emerges from struggles within the Second Temple community of Jerusalem. Its admonitions are explicit. For example, Ezra 10:10 states, "Then Ezra the priest stood up and said to them, "You have acted unfaithfully and married the foreign women, and so you have increased the guilt of Israel." Such rhetoric is decidedly political; it takes sides and is directed toward particular real ends. It simultaneously subverts and supports power arrangements. Because both hearers and speakers participate in constructing meaning, the same rhetoric may communicate different meanings to audiences on opposing sides of a social conflict.

Where marginalized groups deploy public rhetoric to communicate modes of resistance to its members, such rhetoric must speak simultaneously to the interests of the dominant group and to the interests of the subjected group members for the rhetoric to survive publicly. The marginalized group therefore cleverly produces polyvalent rhetoric that possesses both dominant and subversive languages encoded together. The dominant language metaphorically speaks to the interests of the dominant power in the social world, whereas subversive language is encoded within the same rhetoric. The subversive language, which Michel Foucault describes as counter knowledge, signifies the subjected group's history, hopes, and culture in ways that resist repression.[7] Construed this way, the same rhetoric —understood in different ways—

---

[6] Vernon K. Robbins, *Exploring the Texture of Texts: A Guide to Socio-Rhetorical Interpretation* (Valley Forge, Pa: Trinity Press International, 1996), 1.

[7] Reading history as the genealogy of sovereignty and its knowledges that legitimate the crown's public right, Foucault argues that counter knowledges attempt to reverse such claims (*"Society Must Be Defended": Lectures at the Collège de France, 1975-1976*; trans. David Macy [New York: Picador, 2003], 130).

can appeal to groups with opposing interests on opposite sides of a conflict.

Songs such as "Swing Low, Sweet Chariot," sung on antebellum plantations throughout the South, offer an apt example of polyvalent rhetoric:[8]

> Swing low, sweet chariot,
> Coming for to carry me home;
> Swing low, sweet chariot,
> Coming for to carry me home.
>
> I looked over Jordan,
> And what did I see,
> Coming for to carry me home,
> A band of angels coming after me,
> Coming for to carry me home.
>
> If you get there before I do,
> Coming for to carry me home,
> Tell all my friends I'm coming too,
> Coming for to carry me home.

The dominant language of the song was intended for the ears of the white slave-holding class. When Southern planters and their ever-watchful overseers heard African Americans singing this song on Sunday mornings in church and during the workday in the fields, they thought — and were intended to think— that it alluded to the story of the prophet Elijah in 2 Kings 2. It dramatized Elijah's reward for his faithfulness to Yahweh. Elijah's ascension in Elisha's presence signified God's satisfaction with his service. For the slave-holding class, however, the song articulated the slaves' future hope that, after a life-long tenure of acceptable service, God would allow them also to participate in Elijah's heavenly reward.

---

[8] Herbert Robinson Marbury, "Ezra-Nehemiah," in *The Africana Bible: Reading Israel's Scriptures from Africa and the African Diaspora* (ed. Hugh R. Page, et al.; Minneapolis: Fortress Press, 2010), 280-85.

However, within the same rhetoric, the song encoded counter-knowledge to represent an entirely different universe of symbols for African Americans held in chattel slavery. They heard the lyrics and knew that the "sweet chariot" was the Underground Railroad. "Raising" that song in church or in the fields, meant that the "train" was stopping in the vicinity that week or that evening. To "swing low" meant to stop by and pick up new passengers. "Home" was not some spiritual afterlife, but rather life after slavery—that is, life anywhere north of the Mason-Dixon line.[9] The second stanza recalls the Jordan River, the last natural boundary that the Israelites encountered on their forty-year journey to freedom from Egyptian bondage. For African Americans the line between bondage and freedom was the Ohio River, the serpentine extension of the Mason-Dixon line separating slave and free states. To "look over" the Jordan was to envision all who had already escaped to freedom beckoning their sisters and brothers to join them. The meaning of the third stanza is almost self-evident. It acknowledges the rigors and the risks of the journey from slavery to freedom. Not everyone could join the band of escapees. Some were in no condition to make the long, hazardous journey. Some were afraid. Some stayed behind to facilitate the journey for others. The last line, however, articulates a universal hope that all will "get there" someday.

Black preachers and others who deployed the song for political purposes leveraged the multivocal nature of the song's lyrics to create polyvalent meanings in which both enslaved and slaveholder could participate. Both groups participated in their own symbolic worlds of meaning, appropriately constructed to attend to each group's social and political interests. The slaveholder heard the dominant language of the rhetoric and would not have been aware that this rhetoric signaled the arrival of the Underground Railroad and the enslaved person's intent to attain freedom in the here and now rather than in the hereafter. Many held in slavery, who had not read 2 Kings or heard the story of Elijah preached, heard only the rhetoric's subversive language and would not have been aware of another meaning in the lyrics. Only those who

---

[9]After the enactment of the Fugitive Slave Law of 1850, which provided for the forcible return of African Americans who had escaped slavery, blacks were forced to flee to Canada to obtain their freedom.

traveled between both worlds, as enslaved preachers did, understood the song's double significance and why it needed such a polyvalent character to be effective.

The divorce rhetoric composed by the Second Temple priesthood of Jerusalem[10] was likewise polyvalent. Carefully constructed, its dominant and subversive meanings allowed imperial authorities and the Second Temple community to participate in the same rhetorical discourse yet with markedly different understandings and divergent interests. At the political level, the rhetoric signifies the interests of imperial authorities. Its laments and directives articulate a vision of a Second Temple community securely integrated into the imperial system and accepts the state of dominion. This function becomes increasingly important for the empire as it faces war with the Delian League, the prospect of losing Egypt, and the growing conflict with Greek forces during the mid-5th to 4th centuries.

At the cultic level, the rhetoric communicates a counter-knowledge that signifies the interest of the Second Temple priesthood and its community. The rhetoric masks the cult's imperially supported origins and establishes it instead as an institution legitimated by divine authority. In this way, the rhetoric presents the Second Temple priesthood as an extension of Yahweh's power rather than as an

---

[10] I use this term with an awareness of its limitations. First, it signifies a "too-precise" geographic boundary, namely Jerusalem. Clearly, any priesthood centered in Jerusalem would have formal and informal ties and with religious personnel and perhaps even roles outside of Jerusalem. I use the phrase to identify Jerusalem and the temple as its center. Second, while the term "priesthood" references a religious role, any priesthood would operate within several overlapping arenas (political, juridical, economic, and religious, amongst others) within the public sphere. Third, the phrase indirectly signifies a religious identity, Yahwism. However, not all persons in Yehud (or even in Jerusalem for that matter) agreed upon authentic Yahwistic practice. Certainly, archaeological evidence has long demonstrated occurrences of Yahwistic practices integrated with non-Yahwistic practice throughout the Levant. For an exhaustive study of the issues in identifying a specific priesthood such as the Zadokites or Levites, see Alice Hunt, *Missing Priests: The Zadokites in Tradition and History* (London: T&T Clark, 2006).

instrument of the Persian administrative apparatus as were its counterparts throughout the imperial system.

For the Second Temple community, the rhetoric invokes ancient Israel's cultural symbols and stories and participates in the ongoing work of reconstructing for them an identity as a people belonging to Yahweh, not merely subjects of the Persian Empire. In the rhetoric's economic signification, both the interests of the Second Temple community and the imperial authorities elide. The rhetoric's intent, dissolving the exogamous marriages, staves off the loss of *golah* (exiles') land tenure. With rights to arable land, the *golah* have a collective base from which to tithe to the Second Temple. Simultaneously, these tithes enable the temple to meet its tax burden, an obligation no different than that levied against other temples throughout the empire, such as those in Babylonia and Egypt.

Problem: Polyvalent Rhetoric and Univocal Analyses

Scholars have long studied the divorce rhetoric that arose during the mid-fifth century in the Persian province of Yehud attached to the missions of Ezra and Nehemiah.[11] However, the ambiguous messages in

---

[11] Some scholars now locate the literary production of Ezra-Nehemiah in the Hellenistic period. Concerning dating the final form of Ezra-Nehemiah, I agree with the well-argued study by Jacob L. Wright. See Wright, *Rebuilding Identity: The Nehemiah Memoir and Its Earliest Readers* (Berlin: Walter DeGruyter, 2004). However, there is also much agreement that the divorce rhetoric itself reflects the concerns of the Second Temple under Persian rule. These concerns, namely the politics of the rhetoric as it points to power relations between imperial authorities, and the Second Temple community, are the focus of this study. I am not arguing for the historicity of the narratives within Ezra–Nehemiah. To the question of history, two of the more compelling treatments of the Ezra-Nehemiah corpus are those by T. C. Eskanazi and Sara Japhet. In different ways, both approach long-standing historiographical questions through literary analysis. Paying careful attention to literary cues, Eskanazi's study shows convincingly that the text's disjointed chronologies, which had long vexed scholars attempting to use Ezra-Nehemiah for historical reconstruction, were not evidence of a compiler employing incomplete and, in some cases, inaccurate historical records. Rather, by attending to the text's interconnected and repeated themes, Eskanazi demonstrates how these chronologies are subordinate to the writer's primary concerns of communal restoration and law as

the rhetoric   (Ezra 9–10 and Nehemiah 13) have led to different understandings of its intent in the social context of Yehud.

Many studies claimed a univocal, dominant signification of the rhetoric. Arguing that the rhetoric's intent is theological and that its meaning is patently cultic are Julius Wellhausen, Martin Noth, Klaus Koch, David Clines, J. Maxwell Miller and John H. Hayes, Bruce Birch, and Lester L. Grabbe. The rhetoric's concerns, these scholars say, focus on religious purity, Mosaic Law, and priestly ritual.[12] Their treatments see the rhetoric's intent as creating a sacred or theocratic community that arose from an internal need; it only later achieved imperial support, or only incidentally coincided with imperial interests.

For these studies, the rhetoric discloses a religious ideology that held sway in the social matrix of Yehud. Ahlström writes, "Ezra fulfilled

a means of achieving solidarity. See T. C. Eskenazi, *In an Age of Prose: A Literary Approach to Ezra-Nehemiah*, SBLMS (Atlanta: Scholars Press, 1988). Recently, Sara Japhet has authored a learned discussion on discerning historicity in Ezra-Nehemiah, in "Periodization between History and Ideology II: Chronology and Ideology in Ezra-Nehemiah," in *Judah and Judeans in the Persian Period* (ed. Oded Lipschits and Manfred Oeming Winona Lake, In.: Eisenbrauns, 2006).

[12] Martin Noth believed that Ezra's mission attempted to give the religious community in Judah "a new and binding organization since the old tribal federation and its organizations had dissolved…" (*The History of Israel* [New York: Harper and Brothers, 1958], 331-32). Klaus Koch understood Ezra's mission as a means of establishing religious law. For him the divorce rhetoric functioned to make a distinction among the people between the sacred and the profane ("Ezra and the Origins of Judaism," *JSS* [1974]: 173-97). David Clines holds a similar position in *Ezra, Nehemiah, Esther: Based on the Revised Standard Version* (Grand Rapids: Eerdmans, 1984). J. Maxwell Miller and John H. Hayes claim that the separatism signified a religious purity in *A History of Ancient Israel and Judah* (Philadelphia: Westminster, 1986), 472. Bruce Birch appeals to Daniel Smith's argument that the separation signified a concern for ritual purity and an attempt to protect the community from pollution in *Let Justice Roll Down: The Old Testament, Ethics, and Christian Life* (Louisville, Ky.: Westminster John Knox, 1991), 307-9. See also Smith, *The Religion of the Landless*, 139-51. Lester L. Grabbe argues from literary and historical perspectives that the rhetoric indicated a concern for piety and is based on Mosaic Law in *Ezra-Nehemiah* (New York: Routledge, 1998), 143-50.

his most important task: Yahweh's people, the *gola* party, had been firmly established.... Ezra's mission was to establish a theocratic society."[13] Following the narrative to a large degree, they argue that Ezra and Nehemiah returned to Jerusalem because the cult was in disarray, the returnees had neglected the temple, the wall was in ruins, and, most important, the "holy seed" had defiled itself by mixing with the "peoples of the land" (see Ezra 9:2). Devotion to their faith compelled the two reformers to seek the crown's permission to work in Jerusalem. Ultimately, they intended to restructure the community according to the dictates of the Pentateuch, particularly Deuteronomy 6. They generally take up Persia's cooperation with the reformers' plans to carry out such radical social restructuring by one of three explanations: first, the reforms imposed a social order that coincided with Persian interests for internal organization in the provinces; second, Persian kings were benevolent, supportive of religious freedom in the provinces, and tolerant of the religious desires of local cults; or third, the Persians gave the province special dispensation as a reward for remaining loyal to the crown during the revolt of 485 B.C.E. Such a view of Persian political policy discounts Persian interest in the province, and attributes far more autonomy to Yehud than was enjoyed by other provinces under Persian domination. It assumes that the Persian king allowed the radical restructuring of the social world of the most prominent city of the Yehud simply to appease a small minority. It also assumes that the Persian-constructed temple in Jerusalem was a symbol of the king's devotion to or at least patronage of the local cult rather than a part of the regular bureaucratic apparatus that functioned in provinces throughout the empire. In effect, this view reverses the relationship of imperial domination and renders the Persian imperial authorities beholden to the Second Temple priesthood and its community.

Employing later anthropological methods, Joseph Blenkinsopp,[14] T. C. Eskenazi and Eleanore P. Judd,[15] and Daniel L. Smith-

---

[13] Gösta Ahlström, *The History of Ancient Palestine* (ed. Diana Edelman; JSOTSup; Sheffield: JSOT Press, 1993), 889.

[14] Joseph Blenkinsopp, *Ezra-Nehemiah* (ed. Peter Ackroyd; Philadelphia: Westminster, 1988), 173-77, 363-64.

Christopher[16] argue that the rhetoric promotes religious and ethnic identity. They suggest that the rhetoric sets up cultural boundaries by circumscribing markers of ethnic inclusion for the community. The rhetoric protected the *golah* from the Persian cultural hegemony that threatened the Second Temple community's survival. Both these perspectives credit the social and political dynamics internal to the Second Temple community rather than any policy directives of the empire.

Finally, studies by Jon Berquist[17] and Kenneth Hoglund,[18] which extend Peter Frei's[19] hypothesis that the Persian Empire exercised extensive control over Yehud, argue that the interests of the Persian Empire underlie the intent of the rhetoric of the reforms in the books of Ezra and Nehemiah. If this is correct, then the Persian Empire and the exigencies of imperial rule influenced the social organization of the small province more significantly than previous studies admit.

While the rhetoric may validate each of these meanings, all simultaneously operative in the social matrix of Yehud, none functions

---

[15] T. C. Eskenazi and Eleanore P. Judd, "Marriage to a Stranger in Ezra 9-10," in *Second Temple Studies II: Temple and Community in the Persian Period* (ed. T. C. Eskenazi and Kent H. Richards; Sheffield: Sheffield Academic Press, 1994), 266-85.

[16] Smith, *The Religion of the Landless*; Daniel L. Smith, "The Politics of Ezra: Sociological Indicators of Postexilic Judaean Society," in *Second Temple Studies I: Persian Period* (ed. Philip R. Davies; JSOTSup 117; Sheffield: Sheffield Academic Press, 1991); Daniel L. Smith-Christopher, "The Mixed Marriage Crisis in Ezra 9-10 and Nehemiah 13: A Study of the Sociology of the Post-Exilic Judaean Community," in *Second Temple Studies 2: Temple and Community in the Persian Period* (ed. T. C. Eskenazi and Kent H. Richards; JSOTSup 175; Sheffield: Sheffield Academic Press, 1994); Daniel L. Smith-Christopher, "Between Ezra and Isaiah: Exclusion, Transformation, and Inclusion of the "Foreigner" in Post-Exilic Biblical Theology," in *Ethnicity and the Bible* (ed. Mark G. Brett; New York: E. J. Brill, 1996).

[17] Berquist, *Judaism in Persia's Shadow*, 110-19.

[18] Hoglund, *Achaemenid Administration*, 201-40.

[19] Peter Frei and Klaus Koch, *Reichsidee und Reichsorganisation im Perserreich* (Fribourg: Universitätverlag, 1996).

as a univocal dominant signification. The rhetoric is instead, polyvalent; its dominant and subversive intentionalities within the webs of relations of Jerusalem's social world resist analysis by a singular interpretive lens.

The divorce rhetoric signifies within the three arenas of the social matrix of Yehud, namely in the political, the cultic, and the economic arenas. Presenting the rhetoric in this manner attends to the multiplicity of meanings that stem from the rhetoric's intentions. The political signification, its dominant language, is oriented externally, and concerns the geo-political context of Yehud's place in the imperial system. It assures the imperial authorities that the Second Temple community and its deity have accepted the legitimacy of Persian rule and will participate in the empire's program to ruralize the province. The cultic signification articulates counter knowledge internal to the Second Temple community and focuses on the internal politics and dynamics of the province. At the cultic level, the rhetoric employs the power of the ritual and stories of ancient Israel to construct an Israelite identity for those now living in Jerusalem. This identity emphasizes Yahweh's sovereignty over Persian dominion and the Second Temple as a sign of Yahweh's presence rather than an instrument of the Persian bureaucracy. The Second Temple priesthood narrates this counter knowledge to construct a counter history that encourages resistance to imperial domination by cultural fortification. In the economic signification, both dominant and subversive languages work in tandem to fortify the financial resources of the Second Temple. Since the temple's continued functioning depended upon its ability to meet the imperial tax levy, Persian authorities hear in the dominant language a loyal priesthood working to raise the required funds. Its subversive language calls the Second Temple community to support the "house of God" as a counter-knowledge that is essential for the community's cultural and religious survival.

Socio-Rhetorical Critique

Socio-rhetorical critique takes account of two components. "Socio" refers to the thick webs of relations out of which rhetoric arises. "Rhetorical" refers to ways that linguistic signs in a text communicate. In particular, this socio-rhetorical critique attends to the ideological texture of rhetoric, that is to the ways that rhetoric advances or frustrates the interests of particular groups in the social world.[20]

By divorce rhetoric in Ezra and Nehemiah, I refer in this book to rhetoric that warns against exogamy, specifically Ezra 9–10 and Nehemiah 10 and 13. This rhetoric admonishes its hearers against intermarriage by recalling the traditional enemies of Israel found in Deut. 7. While I narrowly circumscribe the divorce rhetoric to include only the sections studied here, rhetoric with similar intent functions throughout the Priestly (e.g., Lev 18:24-29; 20:23) and Deuteronomistic (e.g., Deut 6:14; 7:1-5, 8:20, 23; Josh 24:20; 24:23; Judg 10:16; 19:12) portions of the text.

For the social dimension of the socio-rhetorical critique, I deploy three categories from the Frankfurt School of Critical Social Theory, namely, *legitimation, authority,* and *power*, to attend to the power and influence that the priesthood, the empire, the colonial aristocracy, and the populace exerted upon their shared social matrix, the province of Yehud. *Legitimation* refers to rationalizing or justifying structures.[21] For example, divine law acts as a legitimating structure for the priesthood at the cultic level. Under legitimation, I explore how rhetoric functions within the rationalizing structures of Yehud such as the imperial system or the Second Temple.

Authority refers to agents specified by the rhetoric who have the power to affect certain ends. Under authority, I explore how the divorce

---

[20] By construing rhetorical critique in this manner, I situate my study on a trajectory in Hebrew Bible studies begun by James Muilenburg's seminal article, which argues that the form and content of the rhetoric both work to persuade the hearer ("Form Criticism and Beyond," *JBL* 88 [1969]: 1-18). More recently, Vernon Robbins has added a social dimension to rhetorical critique. Although his study focuses on New Testament texts, his method provides insights for integrating rhetorical study with social theory (*Exploring the Texture of Texts*, 4).

[21] Jürgen Habermas, *Legitimation Crisis* (trans. Thomas McCarthy; Boston: Beacon Press, 1975), 36-37. Raymond Geuss, *The Idea of a Critical Theory: Habermas and the Frankfurt School* (New York: Cambridge University Press, 1988), 15-16, 59. G. E. Lenski, *Power and Privilege: A Theory of Social Stratification* (Chapel Hill: University of North Carolina Press, 1984), 59. Terry Eagleton, *Ideology: An Introduction* (London: Verso, 1991), 37, 54-55.

rhetoric appeals to different agents—specifically the imperial and the priestly authorities—who execute the ends of the empire and the Second Temple community, respectively.

Finally, for the purposes of this study, I employ two conceptions of *power*. Whereas Habermas's concept of *Herrschaft* (repression) describes the nature of imperial domination of Yehud,[22] Foucault's concept of productive power teases out the subtle ways in which power plays a role in ordering the political, cultural, and economic relationships in Yehud. Foucault argues that power resides at every level of society, is everywhere present, and is at work in every encounter between humans. *Herrschaft* turns in on itself, giving way to the possibility of resistance. I use one aspect of Foucault's concept of power to interrogate potential resistance in Jerusalem as disclosed by the rhetoric. For my purposes, this quotation will suffice:

> Power is not something that is acquired, seized, or shared, something that one holds on to or allows to slip away; power is exercised from innumerable points, in the interplay of nonegalitarian and mobile relations.... Power comes from below; that is, there is no binary and all-encompassing opposition between rulers and ruled at the root of power relations, and serving as a general matrix—no such duality extending from the top down and reacting on more and more limited groups.... Where there is power, there is resistance, and yet, or rather consequently, this resistance is never in a position of exteriority in relation to power.[23]

---

[22] Jürgen Habermas and Niklas Luhmann, *Theorie der Gesellschaft oder Sozialtechnologie. Was leistet die Systemforschung?* (Frankfurt: Suhrkamp, 1971), 246-254.

[23] Michel Foucault, *The History of Sexuality Volume 1: An Introduction* (New York: Vintage Books, 1990), 93-94. See also Lawrence D. Kritzman, ed., *Politics, Philosophy, Culture: Interviews and Other Writings of Michel Foucault 1977-1984* (New York: Routledge, 1990), 104-107.

For Foucault, power is almost a totality.[24] In a matrix constituted by power, the activity of imperial domination presumes resistance. The one cannot be present without the other. Power itself is active in the webs of relations in the social world of Yehud. In the rhetorical analysis, I highlight the rhetoric's dominant and subversive languages to demonstrate the limits of *Herrschaft* and its interplay with resistance. In the divorce rhetoric, both forms of power are at play as the Second Temple priesthood assumes postures of acquiescence and resistance. Their rhetorical politics takes the form of counter history, that is, a history whose logic challenges that of the sovereign.[25] No different than the sovereigns of other empires, Persian kings used military power to undergird expansion and enforce their rule. But the crown used propaganda often in the form of narratives to rationalize its rule. For example, the Persian crown's history advertised its benevolence in texts such as the Cyrus Cylinder. In some cases, such as the Verse Account of Nabonidus, it justified conquest by claiming superior administrative capacity to those whom it deposed. It even co-opted local deities and claimed imperial patronage such as in the statue of Udjahorresne or in Isaiah 45:1. These texts intend to unify local populations by engrafting their identities into the history of Persian sovereignty. They mask local narratives of defeat and destruction by characterizing the former power (e.g. Nabonidus and Amasis) as illegitimate. In the history of the sovereign, local populations are expected to claim their place among the grateful subjects who have experienced Persian beneficence. However, in the divorce rhetoric, there is a sophisticated counter discourse that offers a new and cohesive historical alternative. This counter history renders the Second Temple community visible, not as one among the many quiescent multitudes, but as a unique community whose existence in dominion tells a different story of justice and survival.

---

[24] Kritzman, *Politics*, 96-124, especially 124.

[25] Michel Foucault, *"Society Must Be Defended": Lectures at the Collège de France, 1975-1976* (ed. Mauro Bertani and Alessandro Fontana; trans. David Macey; New York: Picador, 2003) 72.

Vantage Point of the Book

While this book attends to the power relations between imperial authorities, the Second Temple priesthood, and the Second Temple community, it does so from the vantage point of the Second Temple priesthood whose perspective offers the reader both an external gaze onto the imperial system and a gaze toward the internal life of the Second Temple community. Each of the three groups—*imperial authorities, Second Temple priesthood,* and *Second Temple community*—offers a different vantage point for analyzing the divorce rhetoric.

The *imperial vantage point* is broad, encompassing the entirety of its conquered territories and their relationship to the central authority. To consider the rhetoric from this position is to ask how the rhetoric's effects might have supported imperial interests on one hand and resisted them on the other. Such an inquiry takes into account Persian interests. For example, the empire needed consistent streams of monetary and in-kind tribute in order to fund military campaigns and local imperial authorities. It needed order, security, and stability for the protection of trade routes between provinces, for the control of volatile borders, and for the quiet rule of local populations and their institutions.

However, the imperial vantage point could account for the internal activity of the provinces, particularly local institutions and cults, only insofar as they related to imperial interests. Imperial authorities would hardly have encountered much of Yehud's population. Such authorities would have collected taxes from the landed aristocracy, which would have included any priesthoods. In other words, the imperial authorities would miss the rhetoric's intention toward fulfilling the interests of the Second Temple community; the rhetoric's appropriation of the signs, symbols, and meanings of a Yahwistic faith; or its appeal to the personalities, themes, history, and culture of ancient Israel. The imperial vantage point could not grasp the relationship between the temple and its community in Jerusalem.

So while an analysis of the effects of the rhetoric from an imperial vantage point would take into account the province's relationship to the central government, its authorities, and its function as a province of the satrapy of Ebr-Nahara, it could not account for the inner dynamics of Yehud's society. Its vantage point would miss the cultic character of the rhetoric and what that dimension might reveal about the priesthood's relationship to the people of Jerusalem.

From the *perspective of the small Second Temple community*, a study of the divorce rhetoric would focus their constitution as a people with a particular relationship to Yahweh. It would take into its purview the community's concern over provoking Yahweh to anger by intermarriage. It would also consider the effect of the mass divorces upon family structures. Such an analysis would also account for community support of the temple as the institution that mediates the power of God and constructs meaning, with regard to historical and geopolitical contexts.

Nonetheless, this vantage point also has its limitations. The gaze from the community's vantage point could not take hold of the relationship between the cult and the empire. Neither could it attend to the meanings of the rhetoric as it regarded the empire's need for cultic legitimation in Yehud, the multifaceted significance of the imperially-constructed temple, or even Yehud's function in the imperial system. Ultimately, the community's gaze looks only inward toward the provincial center (Jerusalem) and upon how local institutions, local officials, local cults, and local economics affected their lives.

A study from the *vantage point of the temple and its priesthood* offers the reader the broadest gaze over the sociopolitical landscape of the province. Located in the province's major urban center, Jerusalem, the Second Temple—Yehud's imperial, cultic, and financial center—sat at the intersection of the three groups. The empire funded its construction and its function for the Persians was no different than other temples in the imperial sphere. At various times over the course of two centuries of Persian dominion, the Second Temple served as a residence for imperial officials (civic and cultic), as an archive for imperial records, as a provincial storehouse for supplies, and perhaps even as a foundry and treasury. It was also, of course, the primary center for Yahwistic worship. The Second Temple priesthood, the group that authored the rhetoric and administered the temple, negotiated the political, cultic, and economic realms of the province from a unique and multifaceted vantage point.[26] In a real sense, the priesthood was "a center" on this periphery of

---

[26] See Blenkinsopp, "Temple and Society in Achaemenid Judah" in *Second Temple Studies 1: The Persian Period* (ed. Philip R. Davies; JSOTSup 117; Sheffield: JSOT Press, 1991). For the general Achaemenid imperial posture toward temples, see M. A. Dandamaev, "Achaemenid Babylonia," in *Ancient*

the empire. In the political arena, the priesthood gazed outward, where it encountered imperial authorities to which it was beholden for the construction of the temple. In the cultic arena, the priesthood's gaze turned inward: it composed rhetoric, established rituals, laws, and boundaries that mediated the very power of Yahweh for the people of the temple community. In the economic arena, the priesthood gazed both inward and outward. Its inward gaze directed the behavior of its adherents to engage in practices that reinforced cultural identity, expressed their Yahwistic faith, and supported the institution's financial needs. Its outward gaze attended to its role as a part of the Persian bureaucracy, and its requirement to meet the imperial tax burden. In each of these arenas, its rhetoric acted as a powerful polyvalent tool, constructing distinct and usually different meanings for the empire and for the people of Jerusalem.

An Outline of the Project

The study begins by describing in chapter two the social world of Yehud with respect to the Second Temple and imperial authorities. Chapters three, four, and five each take up an ideological critique in two phases to attend to both the social context of Persian Yehud and the divorce rhetoric of Ezra-Nehemiah. The first phase offers a thick description of the location of temples in Achaemenid Babylon and Egypt and their function in the wider context of the Persian imperial system. The second phase of the ideological critique analyzes ideological intentionalities of the divorce rhetoric. Specifically, the study analyzes the political and cultic significations of the rhetoric in Ezra 9–10 and the economic significations of the rhetoric in Nehemiah 10 and 13. For each, the analysis attends to the ways the form and content of the rhetoric appropriates structures of legitimation, authority, and power to fulfill the interests of the priesthood, empire, and Second Temple community. The study concludes by attending to two concerns: it analyzes the rhetoric's efficacy at doing ideological criticism first, by examining politics in the social world of Yehud, and second, by examining the motivations of a Second Temple priesthood operating under Persian dominion.

Mesopotamia: A Collection of Studies by Soviet Scholars (ed. I. M. Diakonoff; Moscow: Nauka Publishing House, 1969), 309-10.

Chapter 2

Toward A Construct of Yehud

Economy, Size and Demography, and Identity Construction

We begin by looking at the social world of Yehud with respect to the Second Temple and imperial authorities. The empire developed the province of Yehud at the western frontier of the satrapy of Ebr-Nahara, bordering the satrapy of Egypt to the south, to connect Egypt to the rest of the imperial system. It is important not to overstate Yehud's significance for the Achaemenid Empire. Yehud was a small, poor province, important neither militarily nor economically, but simply because its location during the mid-fifth century placed it within the geopolitical matrix between Egypt and the imperial core.[1] Although it was small, its land hardly productive, and its territory sparsely populated, Yehud still operated in the tight imperial bureaucracy. The character of its Second Temple Community and the rhetoric it produced depended upon real factors such as economic possibilities along with the province's size and demography.

Economy

Two economic issues are relevant for interpreting the divorce rhetoric: First, would such rhetoric make sense given Yehud's material

---

[1] Oded Lipschits, "Achaemenid Imperial Policy, Settlement Processes in Palestine and the Status of Jerusalem in the Middle of the Fifth Century B.C.E.," in *Judah and Judeans in the Persian Period*, (ed. Oded Lipschits and Manfred Oeming; Winona Lake, In.: Eisenbrauns, 2006), 38. See also Pierre Briant, *From Cyrus to Alexander: A History of the Persian Empire* (trans. Peter T. Daniels; Winona Lake, Indiana: Eisenbrauns, 2002), 976.

realities? Second, what evidence is there of imperial influence upon Yehud's economy? Ultimately, the divorce rhetoric emerges from a particular material and social context determined to an important degree by Yehud's economy, size, population, and governing structures.

As it had been under the Babylonians, Persian Yehud operated under a foreign tributary mode of production.[2] By the mid-fifth century, Jerusalem had become the center of several agricultural installations and small villages whose products met the consumption needs of its urban elite. Its wine presses, storage facilities, and olive presses constituted a chain of production of goods as tribute from small villages to Jerusalem.[3] The clear flow of goods and resources from the peasantry to the urban elite is evidence of differentiation in Yehud's economy. Seals, jewelry, and storage containers not of Yehudite origin evidence the urban elite's participation in the larger imperial economy, particularly in trade with other provinces and Greece.[4] Imperial seals show evidence of commerce as taxation or authentication of certain vessels and their contents that met the requirements for tribute.[5] Other than the requirement for tribute, whether the Yehudite economy was "natively" or "imperially" controlled remains open. There is little evidence for imperial direction of Yehud's economy.[6] However, Kenneth Hoglund has argued that imperial military

---

[2] Gale A. Yee, "Ideological Criticism: Judges 17-21 and the Dismembered Body," in *Judges and Method: New Approaches in Biblical Studies* (ed. Gale A. Yee; Minneapolis: Fortress Press, 1995), 150. Norman K. Gottwald, "Sociology," in *ABD* (ed. David Noel Freedman; New York: Doubleday, 1992), 84.

[3] Carter, *Emergence*, 250.

[4] Carter, *Emergence*, 250.

[5] Carter bases his analysis reports on the number and types of seals from nine sites: Jerusalem Bethel, Tel en-Nasbeh, Ramat Rahel, Jericho, En-Gedi, Horvat Zimri, El-Jib, Mosah, and Har Adar. Carter divides these into anepigraphic (with either animal or artistic motifs) and epigraphic (with either *Yehud, Moshah,* or *Phw'*) *(Emergence*, 259-68).

[6] Carter, *Emergence*, 270-71. This statement is based on the small number of Persian coins and the late date to which they are assigned. Carter follows Meshorer's categorization of the forty-one "Yehud" coins into seventeen types. He dates those inscribed in Aramaic to the Persian period, while those inscribed in Paleo-Hebrew script may date to the Persian or Ptolemaic periods. Those

interests had an indirect effect on Yehud's economy, specifically that Ezra and Nehemiah became envoys of Persia. Their missions were examples of imperial responses of military intensification and ethnic collectivization along the western frontiers of the empire.[7] However, Hoglund reinterprets Ephriam Stern's reading of the archaeological record of fortresses constructed on high elevations overlooking major roadway systems in Yehud during the mid-fifth century. Whereas Stern believed that these fortresses protected the borders of Yehud from Edom,[8] Hoglund understands them to have guarded trade routes,

---

dating to the Persian period generally have a defective spelling of the province name, *yhd*, while those which Carter dates to the Ptolemaic period generally are inscribed with a variation of the *plene* spelling *yhdh* or *yhwdh*. Clearly, since his criteria for categorization involve a great deal of overlap, there is room within his schema to date certain coins to either period. The implications of this overlap could be enormous if more Paleo-Hebrew and plene-spelling inscribed coins are dated to the Persian period as his schema allows. See Y. Meshorer, *Ancient Jewish Coinage I. Persian Period through Hasmonaeans* (Dix Hills, NY: Amphora Books, 1982). See also L. Mildenberg, "On the Money Circulation in Palestine from Artaxerxes II till Ptolemy I: Preliminary Studies of Local Coinage in the Fifth Persian Satrapy. Part 5," *Transeuphratène*. 7 (1994): 63-71. Second, the small percentage of Persian coins as compared to those dated to subsequent periods means that Yehud's economy developed slowly. Based on his dating schema (see previous note), Carter organizes data from two sites, Horvat Zimri and the City of David. At the former, the two Yehud coins recovered represent just three per cent of the total. Of the other coins, 53 (39% of the total) were Hasmonean, and the balance he assigns to later periods. At the latter site, of the two hundred twenty-seven coins recovered, only one coin (.4% of the total) dates to the Persian Period coins, 22 date to the early Hellenistic period, and 113 to the Hasmonean period. Carter assigns the balance to later periods. Carter, *The Emergence*, 270.

[7] E. Stern, *The Material Culture of the Land of the Bible in the Persian Period (538-332 B.C.E.)* (Warminster; Wilthsire: Aris & Philips; Jerusalem: Israel Exploration Society, 1982), 245-50. Stern argued that these fortresses protected the borders of Yehud from Edom. Also E. Stern, "The Persian Empire and the Political and Social History of Palestine in the Persian Period" (*CHJ* 1; Cambridge: Cambridge University Press, 1984), 86.

[8] Stern, "The Persian Empire," 96.

protected the commerce that was of vital importance to the imperial economy, and defended the western territories from invasion.[9] For Hoglund, Nehemiah's mission fits well into this context. He contends that Nehemiah's building program, specifically the fortification of Jerusalem, was part of a much larger program of military fortification in Yehud. Both he and Carter argue that as the conquests of later kings (those after Darius) ceased, the need to deplete existing provinces of their economic surplus became more urgent. The need increased markedly as a result of Persia's protracted and costly wars with the Greeks. In later years, more of Yehud's economy would have been focused on the needs of the empire, and more of its wealth siphoned off to imperial coffers. To intensify economic production, Persian authorities encouraged the development of productive agricultural settlements in a program of ruralization along the western frontiers of the empire.

Population and Pluralism

While scholars have generally agreed that Yehud's population increased during the Persian period, the identity and allegiances of the groups that populated the province has remained a question. The excursus below briefly traces scholarly perspectives on the nature of the groups in Yehud, particularly as those groups relate to the province's governing structures.

Excursus:
Internal Governance

Most early studies, although they accepted the historicity of a mass return, assumed internal governance. These studies focused instead on Ezra or Nehemiah priority in terms of instituting internal structures of governance, the nature of the law identified with Ezra, or the historicity of the reformers.

One of the earliest scholars to disagree with the orthodox position was J. D. Michaelis. In 1785, he identified the Persian emperor

---

[9] Hoglund, *Achaemenid Administration in Syria-Palestine and the Missions of Ezra and Nehemiah*, 165-05. See especially 202-05. But see the critique by Lipschits, "Achaemenid Imperial Policy," 37, n.59.

called Artashasta in Ezra 7 as Xerxes, a radically divergent position from the generally argued Artaxerxes I Longimanus.[10] He placed Ezra in Jerusalem in 479 B.C.E. instead of the generally argued 458 B.C.E. His student, Johann Gottfried Eichhorn, in his monumental Old Testament introduction responded by defending the consensus position.[11] In 1868, prevailing scholarly debates took the argument in the opposite direction chronologically, dating Ezra and Nehemiah to Artaxerxes II in 397 B.C.E. and 384 B.C.E. respectively.[12]

By the latter part of the nineteenth century, scholarly debates over these issues had become vigorous and hotly contested. Two spirited and important debates arose during the latter part of the nineteenth-century between A. Kuenen and A. van Hoonaker and later between W. H. Kosters and J. Wellhausen. In 1886, Kuenen defended Ezra-Nehemiah orthodoxy against the more radical positions from Joseph Halévy.[13] Kuenen argued that Ezra was a historical figure, the bringer of the Law, and the founder of Judaism. He identified Ezra's Law as the priestly code.[14] The response that came four years later, when another Dutch scholar, Albin van Hoonacker, published the results of his inquiry into the Ezra-Nehemiah problem, established one of the most influential positions of that and the next era. He argued that the two figures are reversed chronologically in the biblical text so that Nehemiah arrived first in Jerusalem in 445 B.C.E. in the twentieth year of Artaxerxes I (Neh 2:1) and that Ezra arrived in 397 B.C.E. in the seventh year of

---

[10] J. D. Michaelis, *Übersetzung des Alten Testaments mit Anmerkungun für Ungelehrte* (Göttingen: J. C. Dieterich, 1785), 25.

[11] Johann Gottfried Eichhorn, *Einleitung ins Alte Testament* (Leipzig: Weidmanns Erben und Reich, 1787), 560.

[12] Felicien Joseph Caignart de Saulcy, *Étude chronologique des livres d' Esdras et de Néhémie* (Paris: A. Levy, 1868), 41-53.

[13] See Abraham Kuenen, "L'oevre d'Esdras," *RHR* XIII (1886): 334-58. For challenges to orthodoxy, see, Joseph Halévy, "Esdras et le code Sacerdotal," *Revue de l'Histoire des Religions.* IV (1881): 22-45. Joseph Halévy, "Esdras a-t-il promulgué une loi nouvelle?," *Revue de l'Histoire des Religions.* XII (1885): 26-58.

[14] Kuenen, "L'oevre d'Esdras."

Artaxerxes II (Ezra 7:8).[15] Hoonacker met sharp critcism from his
interlocutor, A. Kuenen, [16] but although the two continued their debate
for the next few years, Hoonacker's position held sway in scholarly
circles until well into the twentieth century.

While this debate continued, a new debate arose at the close of
the nineteenth century. Another Dutch scholar, W. H. Kosters, and the
famous German scholar, J. Wellhausen, took up positions on opposite
sides of a similar exchange. In 1895, Kosters argued that Nehemiah
arrives in 445 to rebuild the wall. Realizing that he is short of labor,
Nehemiah returns to Babylon, meets Ezra, and sends Ezra to Jerusalem
in 432. Nehemiah returns to Jerusalem in 434.[17] Wellhausen's response
challenged Kosters's Nehemiah-first position, arguing that Ezra could
have worked in Jerusalem between Nehemiah's missions. He suggested
that Ezra 7:7-8 be emended to read the twenty-seventh year and not the
seventh.[18] Seventeen years earlier in his *Prolegomena*, Wellhausen
depicted the Persian period as a dark age in the history of ancient Israel.
He argued that priestly writers like the Chronicler twisted the facts of
Israelite history for their own ends. For Wellhausen, this era was a time
when priestly religion trumped the natural religion of Yahweh.[19] For
almost a century, Wellhausen's views shaped the attitude of the field
toward the periods of Persian and Hellenistic domination of the Levant.[20]

---

[15] Albin van Hoonacker, "Néhémie et Esdras," *Le Muséon*. IX (1890): 151-84,
317-51, 89-401.

[16] Abraham Kuenen, *Gesammelte Abhandlungen zur biblischen Wissenschaft
von Abraham Kuenen* (Freiburg: J.C.B. Mohr, 1894), 212.

[17] W. H. Kosters, *Die Wiederherstellung Israels in der persischen Perioden*
(trans. A. Basedow; Heidelberg: Hörning, 1895).

[18] Julius Wellhausen, *Die Rükkehr der Juden aus dem babylonischen Exil*
(1895), 166-86.

[19] Julius Wellhausen, *Prolegomena to the History of Israel* (trans. J.S. Black and
Allan Menzies; Atlanta: Scholars Press, 1994), 422-25.

[20] Beginning in 1968, Peter Ackroyd's works initiated a reevaluation of the
Persian period in Hebrew Bible studies. In them, he brings a keen analysis and
an appreciative appraisal to the culture, history, and theology of the Levant.
Peter R. Ackroyd, *Exile and Restoration: A Study of Hebrew Thought of the
Sixth Century B.C* (Philadelphia,: Westminster Press, 1968). Peter R. Ackroyd, *I*

These early studies did not account for Ezra's and Nehemiah's missions as they may have related to the imperial system. In other words, they did not ask how governing structures in Yehud might allow for social and political reforms under Ezra and Nehemiah that served no apparent imperial purpose. Beginning with Albrecht Alt, a trend toward conceiving of Yehud within the imperial system emerges. Alt, Kurt Galling, Ulrich Kellerman, Morton Smith, and J. P. Weinberg represent a line of studies that each in some way gives a narrative of Yehud's achieved autonomy in the imperial system in order to imagine reforms that could proceed without imperial direction. Alt argued that Nehemiah's mission signified a change in the Persian administrative policy of Yehud.[21] The city of Samaria, capital of the Assyrian province of Samarina, had been the dominant governmental center of the region since the period of Assyrian domination.[22] This basic administrative structure remained in place through the period of Babylonian control with Jerusalem and its surrounding territory under Samaria's jurisdiction.[23] For Alt, the political order of Judah changed radically with the arrival of Nehemiah. That Nehemiah directed the program of repopulating Jerusalem (Neh 11:1-2) meant that he had assumed the

---

& II Chronicles, Ezra, Nehemiah (London: SCM Press, 1973). Peter R. Ackroyd, *Israel under Babylon and Persia* (Oxford/New York: Oxford University Press, 1979). Peter Ackroyd, "Archaeology, Politics, and Religion: The Persian Period," *The Iliff Review* 39 (1982): 5-24.

[21]Albrecht Alt, "Die Rolle Samarias bei der Entstehung des Judentums," in *Festschrift Otto Procksch zum sechzigsten Geburtstag* (ed. Albrecht Alt et al.; Leipzig: J. C. Hinrichs, 1934). Reprinted as Albrecht Alt, "Die Rolle Samarias bei der Entstehung des Judentums," in *Kleine Schriften zur Geschichte des Volkes Israel, II* (Munich: Beck, 1953). See also Lipschits, "Achaemenid Imperial Policy," 34-36.

[22] Alt, "Die Rolle," 318-21.

[23] Alt, "Die Rolle," 322, 328-9. To support his hypothesis of the existence and durability of this administrative class over the course of both Babylonian and Persian periods, Alt appealed to the list in Ezra 4:9ff. But his reliance upon an Aramaic ostraca has been challenged in Morton Smith's well-known critique. See Morton Smith, *Palestinian Parties and Politics that Shaped the Old Testament* (New York: Columbia University Press, 1971), 193-201.

governing authority that once belonged to Samaria.[24] Only then, Alt concludes, did Yehud become an autonomous province.

Kurt Galling, a student of Alt's, built on Alt's concept of the relationship between Yehud and Samaria. For Galling, tensions between the two provinces resulted from a disagreement over allowing the colony of Yahu worshipers at Elephantine to construct a temple. He argued, subsequently, that Samaria punished Yehud for its opposition and the intrigue that followed. Regional conflict led to direct Persian intervention. Ezra's arrival was the Persian court's attempt to alleviate some of the financial hardship imposed upon Judah by Samaria, suggested Galling.[25]

Taking cues from both Alt and Galling concerning regional competition and the authority that Nehemiah brought to Yehud, Ulrich Kellerman conceived of two groups populating Yehud: one eschatological and nationalistic, the other priestly and theocratic. He also envisions direct imperial intervention both to appease the local population and to pre-empt an Egyptian threat. Ezra, says Kellerman, returned with a group of the *golah* to Jerusalem to restructure the community according to the dictates of the Law, met with substantial opposition, and failed. He turned to the Passover Papyrus to argue that Samaria's prestige and sway over the community prevented Ezra from enacting his reforms. In the wake of Ezra's departure, the eschatological group attempted to rebuild the wall of Jerusalem. Their efforts also ended in failure, forestalled by external political opposition. Only when Nehemiah arrived with ample Persian authority was the project completed. Kellerman concluded that Nehemiah's mission was initiated

---

[24] Carter, following Peter Machinist's argument, has successfully challenged this thesis in *Emergence of Yehud*, 276-80. See also Peter Machinist, "The First Coins of Judah and Samaria: Numismatics and History in the Achaemenid and Early Hellenistic Periods," in *Achaemenid History VIII* (ed. A. Kuhrt and M. Cool Root; Leiden: Nederlands Instituut Voor Het Nabije Oosten, 1994), 373. Both argue based upon early dating of "Yehud" coins that the province was its own administrative center long before Nehemiah's arrival. Morever, they cite a paucity of Samarian seal impressions in Yehud that date to the Persian period.

[25] Kurt Galling, "Bagoas und Ezra," in *Studien zur Geschichte Israels im persischen Zeitalter* (Tubingen: Mohr, 1964).

by an internal effort on the part of the Jerusalem community who wanted Persian sanction in order to combat Samaritan opposition. As a result, Artaxerxes I agreed to dispatch Nehemiah, a member of his court, to fortify Yehud's defenses in the face of an Egyptian threat. [26]

Focusing more pointedly on internal politics, Morton Smith dismisses imperial interest explicitly, arguing that although Ezra's mission served an official imperial purpose, it failed, and that Nehemiah's mission had no official purpose, only *raisons de coeur*.[27] Nehemiah, as both a "governor" and a leader of the Yahweh-alone party,[28] and having learned from Ezra's failure, first rebuilt the wall using an elaborate program of propaganda and military power, a project that apparently would have been more popular than the religious reforms. More specifically, based on his reading of Neh 4:2 and chapter 5, Smith argues that Nehemiah, in order to stress the urgency of the building project, alleged that neighboring groups were poised to attack Jerusalem, and, where this lacked persuasive force, used the military to conscript laborers by coercion.[29] Next, Smith reads 5:7 and 6:17 as Nehemiah's initiation of a popular economic reform to abolish interest and release peasants from debt. Smith argues that Nehemiah's program was forestalled when he was recalled on the charges of his detractors, who accused him of fomenting revolt.[30] Upon his return, Nehemiah removed from the Temple Tobias the Ammonite, an assimilationist party ally, consolidated power by levying a ten percent tax on all agriculture, and designated the funds for the Levites.[31] This act garnered the Levites'

---

[26] U. Kellerman, *Nehemia: Quellen Überlieferung und Geschichte* (Berlin: Töpelmann, 1967).

[27] Smith makes a distinction between what he calls *raisons d'état* and *raisons de coeur*. He uses Olmstead's discussion of personal favors and the policies the Persian court to support this argument. A. A. Olmstead, *A History of the Persian Empire* (Chicago: University of Chicago Press, 1948), 312. Olmstead, however, is unclear here.

[28] Smith, *Palestinian Parties*, 129.

[29] Smith, *Palestinian Parties*, 130. He bases this on his reading of 4:10.

[30] Neh (12:19 and 6:5ff.). Smith, *Palestinian Parties*, 132.

[31] Neh 13:10-14. Smith, *Palestinian Parties*, 134.

support for the Yahweh-alone party. With a wide and loyal political base in place, Nehemiah began the work of denouncing mixed marriages, the core of the Yahweh-alone platform.[32].

Finally, J. P. Weinberg argued for separate civil and religious authority structures. For years, most scholars of the Persian period accepted and relied upon Weinberg's *Bürger-Tempel-Gemeinde* (*BTG* or Citizen-Temple-Community,) construction of Yehud to account for patterns of urbanization and a coalescing of power in the temples of cities.[33] In the *BTG* Yehud, power was concentrated in the hands of a priesthood, other lesser religious functionaries, and a non-cultic ruling class called a *bet 'abot*.[34] Weinberg argued that postexilic Yehud was a developing *BTG* with Jerusalem becoming the location of the seat of civil authority and of the *golah*. The *golah* competed for status and influence in the province until the arrival of Ezra and Nehemiah.

Weinberg identified two types of citizen-temple communities in the ancient world: those that controlled extensive tracts of land and large temple economies, and those in which all the members of the community participated equally in land ownership. The *BTG* of Judah was the latter type. Its civil and religious realms remained separate until the arrivals of Ezra and Nehemiah. Their administrative tenure signaled a coalescing of the religious and civil authority of the province.[35]

The most contested dimension of Weinberg's arguments is his "two governors" theory. He followed Albrecht Alt, whose argument was accepted at the time Weinberg first published his work. Weinberg argued that in 587 Judah was placed under the jurisdiction of Samaria, and that it only gained full provincial status after the mission of Nehemiah. He believed that the terms *governor* and *prince* referred not only to the governor of the province whose seat of authority was in Samaria but also to the leader of the *BTG*, who gained civil authority over the *golah* community. Weinberg argued that in the wake of the missions of Ezra

---

[32] Smith, *Palestinian Parties*, 135-36.

[33] Joel P. Weinberg, *The Citizen-Temple Community* (trans. Daniel L. Smith-Christopher; Sheffield: Sheffield Academic Press, 1992), 17-33.

[34] Weinberg, *The Citizen-Temple*, 61.

[35] Weinberg, *The Citizen-Temple*, 49-61, 92-104.

and Nehemiah, Yehud became an autonomous province, with the seat of civil authority and the rule of the *BTG* becoming one.[36]

As a result, during the Persian period, Yehud experienced slow, steady population growth. Carter has offered the most precise descriptions of population change over time.[37] For the Persian I period, Carter estimates the population of Yehud to be 13,350 persons, rising to 20,650 persons for the Persian II period. Jerusalem's population numbered around 1,500 people.[38] More recently, Oded Lipschits's study, which envisions a larger Yehud than does Hogland or Carter, does not maintain the distinctions between a Persian I and II period, and estimates the population at 30,125 in the second Persian period. Lipschits suggests that Jerusalem's population increased gradually due to internal cultural concerns rather than due to a "return to Zion," for which he says there is no "imprint on the archaeological date, nor is there any demographic

---

[36] In addition to the problems raised by Alt's thesis, Weinberg's idea of *two* governors recognized by the Persians, operating in the same geographic sphere, has been roundly criticized as impractical and thus improbable. For example, see Peter R. Bedford, "On Models and Texts: A Response to Blenkinsopp and Petersen," in *Second Temple Studies I: Persian Period* (ed. Philip R. Davies JSOTSup 117, ed. Philip R. Davies; Sheffield: Sheffield Academic Press, 1991). See also H.G.M. Williamson, "Judah and the Jews," in *Achaemenid History XI. Studies in Persian History: Essays in Memory of David M. Lewis* (ed. A. Kuhrt and M. Brosious; Leiden: Nederlands Instituut Voor Het Nabije Oosten, 1998), 156ff.

[37] See the critique by Lipschits, "Achaemenid Imperial Policy, Settlement Processes in Palestine and the Status of Jerulalem in the Middle of the Fifth Century B.C.E.," 37, n. 60.

[38] Lipschits, "Achaemenid," 201-2. The majority of the population resided in small villages (2.1 to 5.0 dunams with a population of 51–125 people) or very small villages (0.1 to 2.1 dunams) throughout the Persian period. This small village setting accounted for thirty-seven of the eighty-six sites Carter uses for the Persian period and equaled 43 percent of the population. For the Persian II period, the small village accounted for forty-eight of one hundred twenty-five settlements or 38 percent of the population of Yehud. In both periods, Jerusalem is the only "very large" site (25.1 or more dunams and a population greater than 625) (Lipschits, "Achaemenid," 215-16). His estimates are lower than those of previous scholars (except Albright, who estimates the population at 20,000).

testimony of it.[39] The steady population increase continues until
Jerusalem becomes an urban center in the Hellenistic period.[40] If this is
the case, then of the 1,500 people estimated to have lived in Jerusalem,
only about 200–600 people, or 1-3 percent of Yehud's population, could
be counted amongst its governing and ruling classes. The remainder in
Jerusalem would have been a retainer class of enslaved persons, servants,
scribes, artisans, and others who provided services for the elite. Given
the amount of conjecture, the actual evidence for the increase in
settlements and population in Yehud during the Persian period is less
than helpful in disclosing much about the identity of Yehud's population.

Constructing Yehud

The studies discussed above have done much to illuminate
scholarly understandings. However, because they are based in modern
understandings of identity, many of the proposed categories impose more
on the ancient world than it could have imagined for itself. Two terms
that arise as emic categories offer promise for taking up internal
difference without the surplus of meaning of modern categories: the *bene
ha-golah*, "the children of the exile" or "returned deportees," and those
whom the writers designated the *'am ha'arets,* "the people of the land."[41]

---

[39] Oded Lipschits, "Demographic Changes in Judah between the Seventh and
Fifth Centuries B.C.E.," in Judah and Judeans in the Neo-Babylonian, (ed. Oded
Lipschits and Joseph Blenkensopp; Winona Lake, In.: Eisenbrauns, 2003), 364-
5. Bob Becking has argued convincingly based on his own careful literary
analysis and the existing archaeological data that the mass return should be
described as historical myth. Rather, the evidence shows continuity in the
population of the land of Judah during the Neo-Babylonian and early Persian
periods. The later Persian period shows an increase in population. Following
Hoglund, Becking attributes the rise in population to Persian stimulated trade.
See Bob Becking, "'We All Returned as One!': Critical Notes on the Myth of
the Mass Return," in *Judah and the Judeans in the Persian Period*, ed. Oded
Lipschits and Manfred Oeming (Winona Lake, In.: Eisenbrauns, 2006).

[40] Oded Lipschits, "Achaemenid," 40.

[41] For the purposes of this study, this phrase refers to the small but powerful
landed gentry who rose from the 90 percent of the people who were left behind
during the exile and ascended in power and wealth in the absence of the ruling
classes taken to Babylon (Smith, *The Religion of the Landless*, 179-97). The

The terms' referents are contested throughout the biblical text. Some studies have understood them as identifying class, cultic, and ethnic distinctions. However, modern concepts of ethnicity inadequately convey ancient identity groupings, and so I understand these terms to refer to the two identity forming forces, which I discuss below. Since Persia's "conquest" of Yehud was not violent or destructive as in the case of the Babylonian conquest, the transfer of imperial power initially instituted no clear or decisive change in power arrangements amongst Yehud's population.[42] Persian control initially offered no new predominate cultural expression after the demise of Neo-Babylonian power. Immediately after the Persian "conquest" in Yehud as in much of the satrap of Ebr-Nahara, groups of differing identities, social status, and cultic affiliations continued to compete for resources and power as they had before the Persians arrived. Among others, two identity-forming forces contested with each other: the first, the Yehudite, includes those cultural, religious, political, and economic claims oriented toward the interests, claims, and self-understandings of the local populations of Yehud with Jerusalem at its center; and the second, the Persian, includes those cultural, religious, political, and economic claims oriented toward affirming imperial control.[43] Identities are constructed at the nexus of social forces and group perceptions as imagined possibilities only, not as

---

study also uses this term interchangeably with "inhabitants of the land" and "indigenous people." See a similar use in Robert P. Carroll, "The Myth of the Empty Land," *Semeia.* 59 (1992): 79-91. See also, Ernst Würthwein, "Amos-Studien," *ZAW* 62, no. 1-2 (1950): 10-52. He argues convincingly for this group as landed gentry. But see Lisbeth Fried's insightful study. While referent of the term has generally signified a landed aristocracy, she argues that in Ezra 4:4 that the term refers to Persian officials. Lisbeth S. Fried, "The 'am ha'ares in Ezra 4:4 and Persian Imperial Administration," in *Judah and Judeans in the Persian Period*, (ed. Oded Lipschits and Manfred Oeming; Winona Lake, In.: Eisenbrauns, 2006), 130. If this is so, then any *'am ha-'aretz -golah* intermarriage would mean that the matrix of Persian and Yehudite identity-forming forces is more integrated and complex than recent studies have argued.

[42] Berquist, *Judaism in Persia's Shadow*, 133.

[43] Jon L. Berquist, "Constructions of Identity in Postcolonial Yehud," in *Judah and Judeans in the Persian Period* (ed. Oded Lipschits and Manfred Oeming; Winona Lake, In.: Eisenbraus, 2006), 22.

concrete and fixed quantities. In the social world, however, "identities" are never absolute but are always dynamic and perpetually contested.

On the one hand, the Persian imperial system offered stability and protection from external powers while requiring certain behaviors, ideologies, positions, and loyalties that infringed upon Yahwism. Persian imperial postures offer a clue to the geo-political order even without specific material witness to imperial policy in Yehud. By releasing formerly subjected groups from neo-Babylonian repression with the charge to "return" to a homeland and with imperial backing to reclaim their aristocratic status, the Persians created loyal subjects in Jerusalem and elsewhere who would help them establish a Persian presence in remote regions of the empire. In other words, not only did the Persians want the returnees to attain and maintain power in this western province of the empire; the returnees themselves saw this as an opportunity to gain a measure of power and affluence that they may not have enjoyed in Babylon.[44] Nonetheless, even with the imperial imprimateur, any arriving group found itself pitted against several wealthier and more established groups.

On the other hand, Yehudite identity supported allegiance to particular groups, systems, ideologies, and hierarchies within the province that resisted features of the imperial system in favor of Yahwistic practices of the Second Temple community. Persian and Yehudite identities functioned within a dynamic matrix of other political, ethnic, family, and religious loyalties. As Jerusalem developed politically and economically from the Persian to the Hellenistic periods, so also did the influence of socio-cultural sources (e.g. the Second Temple) for Yehudite identity formation. Any "ethnic" difference between the two is

---

[44] Extant records show that former Judahites were relegated in many cases to agricultural labor. Cornelia Wunsch, "Slavery Between Judah and Babylon: The Exilic Experience," in *Slaves and Households in the Ancient Near East* (ed. Laura Culbertson, Oriental Institute Seminars 7; Chicago: University of Chicago Press, 2011), 117. Many of the exiles in Babylon were unable to maintain their former social and economic standing for lack of education or because of the Babylonians's suspicions of their loyalties. Consequently, many were reduced to the status of peasant farmers. See Niels Peter Lemche, *Ancient Israel: A New History of Israelite Society* (Sheffield: Sheffield Academic Press, 1995), 180.

directly related to the various identity-forming processes, whether imperial or Yehudite.

Conclusion

Although these studies differ in their overall respective configurations of Yehud, they agree in at least two important ways. First, Yehud was a small province with comparatively little economic value to the empire. Its location, aligned directly within the vector of the Persian imperial core's gaze toward Egypt accounted for any imperial attention it received. Since Yehud was not a primary "target" of the imperial machine as were Babylon and Egypt, the Persian "conquest" of Yehud was unlike that of Babylon and Egypt. In both, the Persian imperial presence appeared violently as the result of a military invasion. Yehud's "conquest" was indirect rather than violent or decisive. Its presence just after the fall of the Neo-Babylonian Empire created an immediate political power vacuum instead of readily establishing a new authority. The absence of Babylonian rule only invigorated the ethnic, political and religious rivalries among the various groups within the province. Second, despite its size, Yehud's economy showed evidence of robust participation within the imperial system. Between Jerusalem and outlying areas, the material evidence shows a chain of production of goods consumed by the urban elite and traded with other subjects within the imperial system. The presence of imperial seals is evidence that the province's economic activity had developed sufficiently to be taxed by Persian authorities. Internally, the size of Yehud's economy evidenced social stratification within the province. Peasants labored on lands owned by urban and other elites. Based on the economic evidence, one can surmise the existence of other groups within the rural peasantry and urban elite. Most of the studies referenced above assume the existence of a Jerusalem priesthood and a community of religious adherents.

The question remains: How did these groups, particularly the priesthood in Jerusalem, negotiate their political relationship within the imperial system? Beginning in chapter three, the remaining chapters take up, respectively, the Second Temple priesthood's political relationship with imperial authorities, its cultic relationship with the Second Temple community, and its economic priorities viz. imperial demands and other groups within the province.

Chapter 3

Second Temple Priesthood and Imperial Authorities: Dominant Voice and Political Significations

Uneven Exchanges: Imperial Interests and Priestly Response

The Second Temple priesthood's external gaze toward the imperial authorities, of course, considered the day-to-day exigencies of Persian rule as it impinged upon life in Jerusalem. After 539 B.C.E., Yehud, like Babylon and Egypt after 525 B.C.E., existed as a part of the imperial system. Jerusalem's fortune was tied to the fortunes of the empire and especially to the will of the satrap of Ebr-Nahara. The stern fiscal policy and violent military acts of Cambyses in Egypt; the fiscal generosity, but bureaucratic intensification of Darius I; the reports of Xerxes's destruction of local cults in Babylon; and Artaxerxes I's violent response to Inarus's revolt—all these were a present reality to the priesthood in Jerusalem. These concerns shaped the priesthood's posture toward imperial and provincial authorities who interacted with the temple, checked the nature of its influence over local populations, regulated its income, and levied taxes against it on a regular basis. The rhetoric's political signification responds to the external gaze by affirming the imperial system in Yehud. Imperial realities imposed demands on the Second Temple priesthood just as it had imposed demands on their counterparts in Babylon and Egypt. The priesthood and the empire each had interests that only the other could fulfill.[1] As the Persian Empire sought to compel the Second Temple priesthood's compliance, the Persians already had a successful strategy for imperial legitimation in Babylon and Egypt. From the reign of Darius I forward, chief among the empire's interests for the province was Yehud's security against Greek incursions. For Persia, this threat meant establishing a strong internal understanding that the temple was a cost effective imperial presence.

Imperial Legitimation: Employing Babylonian Cults

When Cyrus II conquered Babylon, he deployed a politically sophisticated set of policies to persuade or coerce temples to cooperate in legitimating Persian rule. In Egypt, Cambyses and Darius repeated this strategy. They utilized religious and royal propaganda coupled with military coercion in Persia's expansionist policy. The heart of this strategy developed useful ties to local priestly elites using an array of tactics. Persian kings granted some elites increased wealth and elevated social status but threatened others with decreased wealth or diminished social status in the new political order. They destroyed some temples and violently deposed their priesthoods, while granting others honored but certainly not powerful political and religious positions. All the while, the Persian imperial system exploited native cultic elites and their familiarity with local customs and religious traditions in order to depict the rule of

---

[1] Gerhard Lenski describes a symbiotic relationship that existed in agrarian societies between the priesthood and the political elites. Each supported the other in gaining advantages of power and privilege. The blessing of the priestly class was essential for the political elite. Only the priesthood could bestow divine legitimation to any governing authority that wished to separate the peasantry from its surplus. At the same time, only the ruling class could offer the priesthood land, military protection, and other forms of wealth (*Power and Privilege*, 260). On the need of the elites for the priestly class, Lenski writes, "The significance of this power to confer legitimacy is difficult to exaggerate." The function of religious ideology here is important not only to the rule of a territory but to the economic functioning of the empire as well.

the new Achaemenid king as a legitimate authority to the local populations.[2]

Empire and Temple in Babylon

Cyrus had long aspired to capture Babylon, but Nabonidus's political blunders opened the door for him to conquer the city. The Babylonian king had so mismanaged his relationship with the priesthoods of Sin and Marduk that he threw his reign into a crisis of legitimation. Nabonidus alienated the powerful priesthood of Marduk with a series of political and fiscal policies that diminished their funding and status.[3] In Marduk's place, he patronized a less influential priesthood, that of the moon deity Sin. Even worse, Nabonidus moved his capital from Babylon, the center for the powerful cult of Marduk, to Teima, his mother's home. For more than a decade while he developed Teima as a religious center for the priesthood of Sin, he neglected his obligations to the cult in Babylon.[4] In the breach, a powerful and politically astute Cyrus forged fruitful relationships with the local disaffected priesthoods.

By the time Nabonidus marshaled his response, he was too late. Cyrus had taken full advantage of Nabonidus's political failings with the competing priesthoods of Marduk and Sin,[5] and claimed to have taken the city in a day without conflict. He took Sippur on October 10, 539 B.C.E. and then the city of Babylon on October 12.[6] Although the Cyrus

---

[2] While the Achaemenids engaged all categories of the aristocracy in this manner, I focus specifically on their engagement of priesthoods and their regulation of local temples insofar as it might illumine the divorce rhetoric. For an in-depth study focusing entirely on the dynamic between the Persian court and temples throughout the empire, see the new study by Lisbeth S. Fried, *The Priest and the Great King: Temple-Palace Relations in the Persian Empire* (Winona Lake, Ind.: Eisenbrauns, 2004).

[3] Paul-Alain Beaulieu, *The Reign of Nabonidus: King of Babylon 556-539 B.C.*, (Yale Near Eastern Researches 10; New Haven: Yale University Press, 1989), 203-17.

[4] Beaulieu, *The Reign*, 149-54.

[5] Beaulieu, *The Reign*, 216-19.

[6] Beaulieu, *The Reign*, 230.

Cylinder collapses the chronology of the conquest of Babylon to a short, almost bloodless, event in the autumn of 539 B.C.E.,[7] the military campaign that led to the conquest began at least two years earlier and was much more of a struggle than the Cyrus Cylinder and other Persian-inspired literature describes.[8] Nabonidus's attempt to relocate sacred statues well in advance of Cyrus's final push to take the city of Babylon suggests that hostilities actually began in the winter of 540–539, much earlier than the Cyrus Cylinder claims.[9] While Cyrus waged a military war on the ground against Croesus in Lydia and then against Nabonidus in Babylonia, he engaged in a much more sophisticated type of warfare using royal and religious propaganda. Particularly, as Kuhrt notes, Cyrus legitimized his conquest of Babylon by manipulating local religious traditions.[10]

In the Cylinder, Cyrus portrays himself as concerned about the well being of the city of Babylon, as a devotee of the cult of Marduk, and as a patron of the neglected priesthood:

> I am Cyrus, king of the world, great king, mighty king, king of Babylon, king of Sumer and Akkad.... When I entered Babylon in a peaceful manner, I took up my lordly reign in the royal palace amidst rejoicing and happiness. Marduk, the great lord, caused the magnanimous people of Babylon [to ...] me, (and) I

---

[7] Among others, Olmstead and Cook follow this portrayal of events. Olmstead, *A History of the Persian Empire*, 49-50. J. M. Cook, "The Rise of the Achaemenids and Establishment of Their Empire," in *The Cambridge History of Iran: Volume 2 The Median and Achaemenian Periods* (ed. Ilya Gerschevitch; New York: Cambridge University Press, 1985), 41ff. But see , 41.

[8] "Achaemenid Inscriptions: Cyrus Cylinder," translated by Mordechai Cogan (COS 2.124). Referring to a report that Nabonidus relocated sacred statues from several Babylonian temples, Briant surmises that this act was intended to prevent Cyrus from capturing them. He suggests that hostilities between the Persians and the Babylonians began as early as the winter of 540 B.C.E., a year earlier than the conquest. Briant, *From Cyrus to Alexander*, 41.

[9] Beaulieu, *The Reign*, 223.

[10] Kuhrt, "The Cyrus Cylinder."

daily attended to his worship. My vast army moved about Babylon in peace; I did not permit anyone to frighten (the people of) [Sumer] and Akkad. I sought the welfare of the city of Babylon and all its sacred centers. As for the citizens of Babylon, upon whom he imposed corvée which was not the god's will and not befitting them, I relieved their weariness and freed them from their service. Marduk, the great lord, rejoiced over my [good] deeds. He sent gracious blessings upon me, Cyrus, the king who worships him, and upon Cambyses, the son who is [my] offspring...[11]

Cyrus arrived in Babylon touting himself as the antithesis of the native king, as one who restored traditions and cultures as opposed to Nabonidus who neglected them. So while Nabonidus acted in devotion to Sin, Cyrus claimed that the Babylonian gods had forsaken Nabonidus and delivered the native king into the Persian conquerer's hands:

Marduk, the great lord, the protector of his people, joyfully looked at his (Cyrus') good deeds and at his (and therefore) ordered him to march against his city Babylon. He made him set out on the road to Babylon going at his side like a real friend...; He delivered into his (i.e., Cyrus') hands Nabonidus, the king who did not worship him (i.e., Marduk).[12]

At every turn, Cyrus was more skillful at deploying a foreign religious tradition than Nabonidus was at using his own native tradition to legitimate his rule. In the end, even Nabonidus's attempt to rescue the gods from Cyrus's advance by transporting statues from local shrines to

---

[11] "Achaemenid Inscriptions: Cyrus Cylinder," translated by Mordechai Cogan (COS 2.124:22b-28). While the Cyrus Cylinder, the Nabonidus Chronicle, and the Verse Account of Nabonidus are all to varying degrees Persian royal propaganda, they demonstrate Cyrus's ability to use religious traditions and cultic elites to legitimate Persian rule. See also Kuhrt, "The Cyrus Cylinder."

[12] Beaulieu, *The Reign*, 225.

Babylon is turned against him. His desperate act of cultic devotion becomes fodder for the reinscribed traditions of cultic elites now loyal to the new dominate power who report that Nabonidus absconded with the gods against their will. In turn, Cyrus strategically claimed to restore these deities to their local shrines:

> From [...], Ashur and Susa, Agade, Eshnunna, Zamban, Meturnu, Der, as far as the region of Gutium, the cities on the other side of the Tigris, whose dwelling-places had [of o]ld fallen into ruin – the gods who dwelt there I returned to their home and let them move into an eternal dwelling. All their people I collected and brought them back to their homes. And the gods of Sumer and Akkad, which Nabonidus to the fury of the lord of the gods had brought into Babylon, at the order of Marduk, the great lord, in well-being I caused them to move into a dwelling-place pleasing to their hearts in their sanctuaries. May all the gods, whom I have brought into their cities, as before Bel and Nabu for the lengthening of my life, say words in my favor and speak to Marduk, my lord: 'For Cyrus, the king, who honours you, and Cambyses, his son....[13]

In exchange, the Persian king received the loyalty of the local populations, or at least the public support of local priesthoods and other elites. The "Verse Account of Nabonidus" gives an version, in similar fashion, of the same pro-Persian propaganda:

> [...] fortifications he has built on Imgur-Enlil.
> [...] male and female (divine statues) he has returned to their shrines. [...] who had left their [...], he has returned to their sanctum.
> [...] he has calmed, their spirits he has gladdened,

---

[13] Amélie Kuhrt, *The Persian Empire: A Corpus of Sources from the Achaemenid Period* (2 vols.; vol. 1; 2007), 72-3.

[…] those who had been brought low, he has brought back to life.[14]

Presumably Babylonian cultic elites, versed in local religious traditions and disenfranchised by Nabonidus's policies, composed these traditions in order to demonstrate their loyalty to the new dominant power. They were anxious to reap whatever benefits were to be gained by ingratiating themselves to the new ruler.

Cyrus's strategy was ultimately successful in Babylonia. Engaging local cultic elites enabled him to enlist them, by either persuasion or coercion, to generate propaganda that would make Persian imperial dominion acceptable to the surrounding communities.

Imperial Legitimation: Employing Egyptian Cults

In Egypt, Cambyses and Darius I repeated Cyrus's successes. By the year 525 B.C.E., Cambyses had ruled for five years. His far-flung empire needed new sources of income. Even though it would be difficult to rule, Egypt looked promising as a new source of imperial wealth. However, Egypt's history of short-lived submission, resistance, and then outright rebellion would trouble any ambitious ruler who aspired to conquer. For example, two centuries earlier, the Nubians, under the Napatan kings, dominated Egypt, but had to retreat.[15] A century later (674–664 B.C.E.) the Assyrians, first under Esarhaddon, and later under Ashurbanipal, asserted control but ruled only intermittently as they competed with the Nubians for power. By 656 B.C.E., Egypt once again achieved autonomy under the new Saïte dynasty in the person of Psammetichus I. His father, Necho I, had ruled as a client-king of the Assyrians.[16] In short, Egypt never submitted for long; any empire occupying it did so in the face of great resistance, which meant huge expenditures of monetary and military resources. Persia, however, employed another tool in its attempt to dominate the wealthy North African nation. Just as it had done in Babylon fourteen years earlier,

---

[14] Kuhrt, *The Persian Empire,* 77-8.

[15] Amelie Kuhrt, *The Ancient Near East c. 3000-330 BC* (ed. Fergus Millar; 2 vols.; vol. 1; New York: Routledge, 1995), 632-33.

[16] Kuhrt, *The Ancient Near East,* 1:634-38.

Persia turned to a strategically constructed royal ideology to legitimate imperial rule.

Conquering Egypt might have proven more difficult for Cambyses had not a young and inexperienced Psammeticus III recently ascended the throne. By midsummer of 525 B.C.E., Cambyses solidified his power in Egypt and established himself as "King of Upper and Lower Egypt."[17] After the Persian conquest, as it was before the arrival of the Persians, the Pharaoh reigned over all; however, this time he was a foreigner and a ruler in absentia. To persuade the Egyptians to accept this new type of rule from a foreign and absentee pharaoh, the Persians constructed a royal ideology that represented Persian pharaohs as native pharaohs. Persian pharaohs eagerly represented themselves as legitimate successors to the throne. Both Cambyses's and Darius's policies in Egypt portrayed the Persian kings as legitimate Egyptian pharaohs.

Following Cyrus's practices in Babylonia, Cambyses and Darius I directed the priesthood of the sanctuary of Neith at Saïs to represent Persian kings as legitimate descendants of the Saïte kings. They developed formal alliances with temples and cultic elites. On his statue, which originally was placed in the temple of Neith at Saïs in the third or fourth year of Darius I, Udjahorresne reported that Cambyses instructed him to create grand royal titles in the style of the Saïte kings. In return, Udjahorresne claimed that Cambyses rid the temple of foreign soldiers, ordered its purification, restored land to the sanctuary of the goddess of Neith at Sais, and established libations for Osiris:

> I asked the majesty of the King of Upper and Lower
> Egypt Cambyses on account of all the foreigners who
> had set themselves down in the temple of Neith should
> be expelled therefrom in order to cause that the temple
> of Neith should be once more in all its splendor as it had
> been earlier. Then his majesty commanded to expel all
> the foreigners who dwelt in the temple of Neith, to tear

---

[17] "Statue Inscription of Udjahorresne" (Miriam Lichtheim, *Ancient Egyptian Literature* [Berkeley and Los Angeles: University of California Press, 1980], III: 38). See also Kuhrt, *The Persian Empire: A Corpus of Sources from the Achaemenid Period*, 118.

down their houses and their entire refuse which was in
the temple. His majesty commanded to purify the temple
of Neith and to restore to it all its people [...] and the
hourly-priest of the temple. His majesty commanded that
offerings should be given to Neith, the Great One, the
Mother of God, and to the great gods who are in Sais as
it was earlier in it.... The King of Upper and Lower
Egypt came to Sais.[18]

This narrative inscribed upon the statue is a brilliant piece of Persian
propaganda that seized upon the legend of Apries according to which
Cambyses, the direct descendant of Apries, had come to Egypt to avenge
the death of his father and his betrayal by Amasis.[19] Those subjects still
loyal to the memory of Apries would have supported Cambyses's rule
over the "usurper" Amasis.

Darius, Cambyses's successor, followed the practice of exploit-
ing relationships with local priesthoods to represent himself as a native
pharaoh. The statue of Udjahorresne names Darius the "Great Chief of
Every Land, Great Ruler of Egypt." In return, Udjahorresne reported that
Darius elevated him to be chief physician of the "House of Life."[20] He
bestowed upon Darius the traditional pharaonic title, "Lord of the Two
Lands." At the sanctuary at El-Kharga, Darius completed the temple's
construction. In return, there are two pharaonic throne names ascribed to
Darius I found at the temple there.[21] The inscriptions praise Darius's
prowess as a builder and extol him as one favored by Amon Ra and

---

[18] Kuhrt, *The Persian Empire*, 118.

[19] Herodotus, *The History*. III.2 (Greene).

[20] "Statue Inscription of Udjahorresne" (Lichtheim, 39). See also Kuhrt, *The Persian Empire*, 118-19.

[21] Herbert Eustis Winlock, ed., *The Temple of Hibis in El Khargeh Oasis* (New York: Arno Press, 1941), 7-9. While the temple's construction began under the last of the Saïte kings, the bulk of the work has been dated to the reign of Darius. There, he is called the son of Re.

Horus. Other reliefs along the wall of Hibis at El-Kharga connect Darius's rule to the power of the gods.[22]

Among Darius's many building projects in Egypt was the canal between Bubastis and the Red Sea.[23] Herodotus reports that Necho began construction of the canal but that "Darius, the Persian" completed it.[24] Diodorus gives much the same report.[25] On the stelas marking the construction of the canal and recalling its builder, Darius is named as the rightful ruler and legitimated by the power of the gods: "Born of Neith, mistress of Sais... He whom Ra placed on the throne to finish what he started. His mother, Neith, bestowed the bow upon him to [repel] his enemies every day as she had done for her son, Ra."[26] The inscription on the statue placed at the entrance of the so-called Darius Gate located at Susa goes even further to vest Darius's reign with the authority of the gods.[27] In these public spectacles, the priesthood affirmed Persian rule for local populations.

Patterned after Cyrus II the Great in Babylonia, Cambyses and Darius's politically sophisticated postures developed ties to local elites either by creating a royal ideology that the elite would support or by granting them increased wealth. The Achaemenid kings granted elites honored, but not powerful, political positions[28] and exploited their connections to the elite and their familiarity with local customs and cultures in order to make the kings' roles acceptable to the local

---

[22] J. Yoyotte, "Les inscriptions hiéroglyphique: Darius et l'Égypt," *Journal Asiatique* 260, no. 3-4 (1972): 253-56.

[23] Herodotus, *The History*. II.158–59 (Greene).

[24] Herodotus, *The History*. II.158–59 (Greene).

[25] Diodorus, *Library of History*. II.33 (Oldfather, LCL).

[26] Briant, *From Cyrus to Alexander: A History of the Persian Empire,* 478.

[27] Yoyotte, "Les inscriptions hiéroglyphique: Darius et l'Égypt."

[28] Udjahorresne, who was the architect of Cambyses's and Darius's royal ideologies in Egypt, was effectively demoted from his position as military commander of the royal navy under the Saite kings to "Chief physician" of the temple at Neith. The biographical inscription on the statue describes his duties and new roles under the Persians. Most involve honoring the two Persian kings and publicizing their patronage.

populations. We can see from the statue of Udjahorresne that this included using traditional pharaonic titles and patronage of Egyptian gods to mold an image emulating a native Egyptian pharaoh. Clearly, Persian imperial rule took great interest in engaging temples in both Babylon and Egypt. Using a varied array of tactics, Persia forged alliances with, or coerced cooperation from, local temples, all with a view toward closely governing the provinces.

Imperial Legitimation and the Jerusalem Second Temple Priesthood

In Yehud, the need for security was paramount for the empire. Both the repeated revolts by a restless Egypt and the increasing number of incursions by Greek forces posed serious external threats to the province. By the mid-fifth century the threat of the Delian League in particular presented a serious crisis for the empire. Had Artaxerxes I allowed Egypt and the Delian League to defeat Persia at Memphis, the empire might have lost the entire Mediterranean corridor. In response to its need to secure its western frontier, Persia sought to integrate more securely the populations settled along its western border.[29] This threat and the comcomitant need for security only intensified as the wars with the Greeks raged on until the demise of the Persian sovereignty in 332 B.C.E.[30] Social order in the province was essential to maintain security.

---

[29] Hoglund, *Achaemenid Administration in Syria-Palestine and the Missions of Ezra and Nehemiah*, 165-205, especially 203-205. For Hoglund, political, ethnic and geographic boundaries intersect where the security of the empire was at stake.

[30] The far-flung and protracted war against the Greek city-states was increasingly burdensome to the imperial economy. That cost would have been passed on to the provinces as increases in requests for agricultural products to supply provisions for the military, increases in monetary requests for salaries, and possibly even land grants made to Persians soldiers and foreign mercenaries, as were made in Egypt or Babylon. Berquist argues that beyond the costs of war, trade between the Levant and the Greek city-states impoverished the province of Yehud. "Trade became increasingly important throughout the Persian period and Yehud was forced to barter because of its lack of silver money" (Berquist, *Judaism in Persia's Shadow*, 109). He argues that interest rates in Yehud may have been as high as 12.5%, while more generally interest rates were as high as 40-50%. See also Stolper, who argues that while the Persians extracted great

Persia could not afford volatility within the populations occupying any of the provinces located along this strategically important western border of the province. Yehud's location, just east of the *via maris* positioned it close enough to trade and military routes to Egypt and to the Mediterranean Sea to make its social organization important for Persia and to push Persia to maintain its military supply lines and commercial trade routes to Egypt.[31] On its expeditions to Egypt, the imperial army likely relied upon Yehud for provisions, and this need pushed Yehud to intensify its agricultural production.[32] Such imperial interests needed an organized group with a strong sense of cultural identity and political loyalty to spearhead its support, a group whose cultic leadership was strategically tied to the imperial system.

Finally, to legitimate Persian rule in the province, the empire needed support from the Jerusalem cult, something only the priesthood could give. Persia had gained local priestly support in Babylon and in Egypt by constructing temples and other cultic artifacts. The Persians, no doubt, would expect the same of the temple constructed in Yehud. Funding the construction of a temple in the late 6th century B.C.E. cemented Persia's relationship with the Jerusalem temple and its community. With an imperially funded temple, its priesthood would gain ascendancy in the province. The temple was the most imposing construction in Yehud. With imperial legitimacy, the temple and its priesthood could eradicate other local religious centers, which might

---

amounts of silver from its provinces, there was no shortage of silver in Babylonia. See *Entrepreneurs and Empire: The Murasu Archive, the Murasu Firm, and Persian Rule in Babylonia* (Uitgaven van het Nederlands Historisch-Archaeologisch Instituut te Istanbul; Istanbul: Nederlands Historisch-Archaeo-logisch Instituut te Istanbul, 1985), 144-46.

[31] Hoglund, *Achaemenid Administration*, 202.

[32] Berquist, *Judaism in Persia's Shadow*, 60-66. Berquist also reads Haggai 2 as response to Persian military presence in Yehud. Arguing that the prophet sought to address the arrival of Darius I and his army, Berquist suggests that Haggai sought to pacify the apprehension of the community and entreat them to meet imperial military needs by intensifying the agricultural production of the small colony. See also Briant, *From Cyrus to Alexander*, 577.

siphon off potential resources in the form of tithes.[33] The empire's temple, however, meant that any priesthood occupying it was beholden to the imperial system in a particular way. [34]

Persia's relationship with the Jerusalem temple took the form of a network of exchanges, replicating its relationship with temples in Babylonia and Egypt. The empire took great interest in cults in those territories, and was greatly invested in the ideology promulgated by the Jerusalem temple. In return for the Jerusalem temple community's compliance, the empire could provide the temple with gifts that only the ruling class could bestow. These gifts were few and rare. Furthermore, the satrap could take away these gifts at any moment. For its part, the imperial system provided the Jerusalem priesthood with funds to construct a temple. However, the empire could also easily destroy it— as it had done to other temples and cultic shrines. The empire also provided cults with stability.[35] Although imperial rule was oppressive, life under the Persians was peaceful. With the stability provided by imperial order came the assurance that the calamity of 587 B.C.E. would not occur again. In return, the temple in Jerusalem provided some legitimacy for imperial rule. Where Cyrus was Marduk's emissary in pro-Persian religious propoganda, Deutero-Isaiah named Cyrus as Yahweh's

---

[33] W. E. Claburn argues that the strategy behind Josiah's reforms was to centralize the cult and direct financial support to Jerusalem, the seat of political power, where he might exert greater control ("The Fiscal Basis of Josiah's Reforms," *JBL* 92:1 [1973]: 11–22). The construction of the Second Temple, centralizing the cult in Jerusalem would do the same for the Yehudite priesthood.

[34] "The support of the political elite proved valuable in yet another way. Few members of the priestly class did not seek to honor God with splendid temples, statues, and works of art, all of which were extremely costly. Here, again, the political elite was singularly equipped to satisfy this desire. In short, there was a natural basis for a symbiotic relationship between these two classes" (Lenski, *Power and Privilege*, 261).

[35] Although regional and ethnic competition ensued, there still existed the overarching political stability of the imperial system. John H. Kautsky, *The Politics of Aristocratic Empires* (New Brunswick, NJ: Transaction Publishers, 1997), 111.

messiah.[36] The Hebrew Bible extols the Persian king's conquest of Babylon as Yahweh's activity on Israel's behalf. In a more sustained manner, the divorce rhetoric discussed below invests Persian rule with divine sanction and directs the community to accept the new order.

Analyzing the Rhetoric: Assurance to the Empire

The Second Temple priesthood, as both imperial officials in the Persian bureaucracy and temple officials of the Yahwistic community in Jerusalem, played an important role in the connection between external security and internal order. As local cultic officials, they developed the rituals and constructed the rhetoric under which imperial dominion was acceptable. In this regard, the Second Temple priesthood acted in the same way as other temple priesthoods throughout the Persian Empire. Analogous to antebellum spirituals, the rhetoric in Ezra 9 speaks both a dominant, or sovereign, and a subversive, or counter, language. Its dominant language, the political signification of the rhetoric, affirms the interests of imperial authorities and calls the Jerusalem population to accept the political realities of imperial control.

Author's Translation of Ezra 9–10

Ezra 9

1. At the end of these things, the officials drew near to me saying, "The people of Israel, the priests, and the Levites have not separated themselves from the peoples of the lands and their abominations from the Canaanites, Hittites, the Perizzites, the Jebusites, the Ammonites, the Moabites, the Egyptians, and the Amorites.[37]

2. For they have taken some of their daughters (as wives) for themselves and for their sons. The holy seed has mixed itself with the peoples of the lands and the hand of leaders and the chiefs have led the way.

3. When I heard this word, I rent my garment and my cloak and pulled hairs from my head, my beard, and I sat appalled.

---

[36] Isa 45:1

[37] Some Hebrew manuscripts and the LXX read "the Edomites" for "the Amorites." Both appear in lists of the traditional enemies of Israel. Cf. Deut. 7:1 and Deut. 23:3ff.

4. And all those who trembled in awe on account of the words of the God of Israel, concerning the unfaithfulness of the golah, gathered around me as I sat appalled until the sacrifice of the evening.

5 At the evening sacrifice, I got up from fasting with my cloak and my garments torn, and fell upon my knees and spread my hands to Yahweh, my God.

6. And I said, "I am too ashamed and humiliated to lift my face to you my God, for our iniquities have risen above the tops of our heads, and our guilt has expanded to the heavens.

7. From the days of our ancestors until this day, we have been in great guilt and for our iniquities, we, our kings, and our priests have been placed in the hand of the kings of the lands, to the sword, to captivity, to plundering, and to utter shame, as it is this day.

8. And now, for a moment, favor has been shown to us by the Lord, our God, to leave for us an escaped remnant to give to us a stake in this holy place, so that our God may lighten our eyes and sustain us in our enslavement.

9. For we are slaves, and in our enslavement, our God has not forsaken us but has stretched out to us kindness before the kings of Persia to give to us life,[38] to raise up the house of our God, to repair its ruins, and to give to us a wall in Judah and in Jerusalem.

10. And now, what shall we say after all of this, our God, for we have forsaken your commandments

11. which you commanded by the hand of your servants the prophets, saying the land which you are entering to possess is a land that is abhorrent with the pollutions of the peoples of the lands and their abominations, which fill it from end to end in uncleanness.

12. And now, do not give your daughters to their sons and do not take their daughters for your sons, and do not seek their peace or their goodness forever, so that you may be strong and eat from the good of the land and cause your children to inherit it forever.

13. After all that has come upon us for our evil deeds and our great guilt, you, our God, have held back our punishment and given to us a remnant[39] such as this.

---

[38] Literally, "sustenance."

[39] Literally, "deliverance, escape."

14. Shall we break your commandments and marry with the people who commit these abominations? Would you not be angry with us until you finish us off without a remnant or a survivor?

15. O Lord, God of Israel, you are just, for we have escaped as a remnant as it is this day. Here before your eyes is our guilt, for there is no one who can stand before you for this."

Ezra 10

1. And as he prayed and confessed, throwing himself before the house of God, a great assembly of men, women, and children gathered around him from Israel, for the people wept greatly.

2. And Shecaniah, son of Jehiel, of the descendants of Elam, said to Ezra, "We have been unfaithful with our God and (caused the foreign women from the people of the land to dwell [with us]) married the foreign women from the people of the land. But now there is hope for Israel, in spite of this.

3. "So now let us covenant with our God to drive out all the wives[40] and their children, in accordance with the counsel of my lord[41] those who tremble at the commandment of our God. So according to the law, let it be done.

4. Arise, for the obligation[42] is upon you. We are with you. Be strong. Do it!"

5. So Ezra arose and made the leading priests, the Levites, and all Israel swear to do as had been said. So they swore.

6. Then Ezra got up from before the house of God and went to the room of Jehohanan, son of Eliashib, where he spent the night.[43] He did not eat bread, nor did he drink water, for he was in mourning over the faithlessness of the golah.

---

[40] The MT reads "all women" while 1 Esdras 8:90 reads "all our wives of an alien race." That only foreign wives is meant here is clear from verse 2.

[41] MT refers to the deity. Here I read *adonai* referring to Ezra, with 1 Esdras and some Hebrew manuscripts.

[42] Literally, "word."

• [43] The MT reads "And he went there." This is most probably a scribal error. The LXX reads "And he dwelt there." Most likely the LXX *Vorlage* read ‏ו‎ and scribal error mistook the final ‏ו‎ for a final ‏ך‎.

7. And the utterance went throughout all Judah and Jerusalem, and to all of the children of the golah, to gather in Jerusalem.

8. And all who did not come within three days, according to the counsel of the officials and the elders, all of their property would be devoted to the ban, and they will be separated from the congregation of the golah.

9. Then all the people of Judah and Benjamin gathered in Jerusalem within three days. It was the ninth month on the twentieth day of the month, and all the people in the plaza of the house of God, trembling, because of this matter, and because of the deluge of rain.

10. Then Ezra the priest stood up and said to them, "You have acted unfaithfully and married the foreign women, and so you have increased the guilt of Israel.

11. "Now give thanks to the Lord, the God of your ancestors, and do his will; separate yourselves from the peoples of the land and from the foreign wives."

12. And all the assembly answered in a loud voice, "It is so. It is upon us to do as you have said."

13. But the people are many, and it is the time of the rains; so we cannot stand outside. And this is not a matter for one day or two days, for many of us have rebelled in this matter.

14. Pray, let our officials stand for the entire congregation, and let all who have taken foreign wives come at appointed times along with the elders and judges of the city, until the fierce anger of our God has been turned away from us on this matter."

15. Only Jonathan son of Asahel and Jahzeiah son of Tikva stood against this, and Meshullam and Shabbethai, the Levites, supported them.

16. Then all the children of the golah did so. And Ezra, the priest, set apart[44] men, heads of the households, according to their families each by name. On the first day of the tenth month, they sat down to examine the matter.

17. They had ended all of the men who married foreign women by the first day of the first month.

---

[44] Reading the LXX, "And Esdras chose for himself leading men...."

18. Of the descendants of the priests who had married foreign women were the descendants of Jeshua son of Jozadak and his brothers: Maaseiah, Eliezer, Jarib, and Gedaliah.

19. They set their hands to send away the foreign wives, and their guilt offering was a ram of the flock for their guilt.[45]

20. Of the descendants of Immer: Hanani and Zebediah.

21. Of the descendants of Harim: Maaseiah, Elijah, Shemaiah, Jehiel, and Uzziah.

22. Of the descendants of Pashur: Elioenai, Maaseiah, Ishmael, Nethanel, Jozabad, and Elasah.

23. And of the Levites: Jozabad, Shimei, Kelaiah, (who is Kelita), Pethahiah, Juday, and Eliezar.

24. Of the singers: Eliashib. Of the gatekeepers: Shallum, Telem, and Uri.

25. And from Israel, from the descendants of Parosh: Ramiah, Izziah, Malchijah, Mijamin, Eleazar, and Hashabiah.[46]

26. And from the descendants of Elam: Mattaniah, Zechariah, Jehiel, Abdi, Jeremoth, and Elijah.

27. And from the descendants of Zattu: Elioenai, Eliashib, Mattaniah, Jeremoth, Zabad, and Aziza.

28. And from the descendants of Bebai: Jehohanan, Hananiah, Zabbai, and Athlai.

29. And from the descendants of Bani: Meshullam, Malluk, Adaiah, Jashub, Sheal, and Jeremoth.

30. And from the descendants of Pahath-moab: Adna, Chelal, Benaiah, Maaseiah, Mattaniah, Bezalel, Binnui, and Manasseh.

31. And from the descendants of Harim: Eliezer, Isshijah, Malchijah, Shemaiah, Shimeon,

32. Benjamin, Malluch, and Shemaiah.

33. And from the descendants of Hashum: Mattenai, Mattattah, Zabad, Eliphelet, Jeremai, Mannaseh, and Shimei.

34. And of the descendants of Bani: Maadai, Amram, Uel,

35. Benaiah, Bedeiah, Cheluhi,

36. Vaniah, Meremoth, Eliashib,

---

[45] See 1 Esdras 9:20 (LXX).

[46] See 1 Esdras 9:26 (LXX).

37. Mattaniah, Mattenai, and Jaasu.

38. And of the descendants of Bani,[47] Shimei,

39. Shelemiah, Nathan, Adaiah,

40. Machnadebai, Shashai, Sharai,

41. Azarel, Shelemiah, Shaemariah,

42. Shallum, Amaraiah, and Joseph.

43 And from the descendants of Nebo: Jeiel, Mattithiah, Zabad, Zebina, Jaddai, Joel, and Benaiah.

44. All these had taken foreign wives, and they sent them away with their children.[48]

The dominant language, the political signification of Ezra 9-10, proceeds in three rhetorical moves. The first move, in Ezra 9:3-7a, indicts the Second Temple community with an act against Yahweh so egregious that the community no longer has any moral ground on which to stand; the community becomes constituted by overwhelming guilt. The second move proceeds to judgment in 9:7b. The rhetoric holds the community responsible for their current political state and grounds Persian rule with divine legitimation. This guilt motif preemptively trumps any complaint against imperial repression. It usurps the moral ground for their dissatisfaction. The third move from 9:8ff encourages the community to participate in the program of ruralizing (increasing the agrarian productivity of) this western frontier of the empire to which they have been deported. Taken together, these three moves affirm a sovereign narrative that portrays local populations as potential legitimate subjects who need imperial deliverance in the person of the Achaemenid king. At the level of political discourse, the rhetoric, though cast as a memoir,[49] is probably better understood as a scripted dialog between the priesthood and the populace, a dialog in which the people give tacit assent to the intent of the rhetoric by way of specific, programmed

---

[47] The MT and LXX read Bani. However, this probably a scribal error and should read Binnui.

[48] See 1 Esdras 9:36. Meaning of the MT is uncertain here.

[49] Clines, *Ezra, Nehemiah, Esther*, 6ff. H. G. M. Williamson, *Ezra, Nehemiah* (Waco, TX: Word Publishing, 1985), 20.

responses. Nonetheless, the "absences,"[50] cracks, and fissures in the rhetoric disclose dissenting voices resisting the legislation against intermarriage.

With three symbolic acts, Ezra's dramatic performance signifies his utter anguish because of the guilt of the temple community over "this thing"—the mixed marriages. Ezra rends his garment and his cloak, pulls hair from his head and beard, and sits appalled. The tearing of his garments (in v. 3) recalls similar acts in other postexilic texts[51] (Job 1:20; 2:12), while the shaving of one's head recalls the exilic prophetic tradition in Jer 41:5.[52] In both the Job and Jeremiah texts, the symbolic acts signify great lament. By performing acts associated with the Job and Jeremiah traditions, the rhetoric connects Ezra's public mourning to traditions already established in the collective memory of the community.[53] In this series of familiar symbolic acts, the rhetoric

---

[50] Terry Eagleton, *Criticism and Ideology* (London: Verso, 1982), 72.

[51] Job 1:20. Then Job arose, tore his robe, shaved his head, and fell on the ground and worshiped. Job responds in anguish to the report of the loss of his sons and daughters. In Job 2:12, the response of his friends upon seeing Job's distressed state is similar, "When they saw him from a distance, they did not recognize him, and they raised their voices and wept aloud; they tore their robes and threw dust in the air upon their heads." Blenkinsopp identifies Ezra's behaviors as "conventional expressions of mourning." See Blenkinsopp, *Ezra-Nehemiah,* 177. Similarly, Clines note that Ezra's acts are customary behaviors associated with mourning (Clines, *Ezra, Nehemiah, Esther,* 120).

[52] After the murder of Gedeliah, Jer 41:5 reports, "eighty men arrived from Shechem and Shiloh and Samaria, with their beards shaved and their clothes torn, and their bodies gashed, bringing grain offerings and incense to present at the temple of the LORD."

[53] Gottwald, among others, dates Jeremiah's prophecy from 609 (the Death of Josiah) to 587 (the destruction of Jerusalem). Norman K. Gottwald, *The Hebrew Bible: A Socio-literary Introduction* (Philadelphia: Fortress Press, 1985), 395-96. See also John Bright, "The Date of the Prose Sermons in Jeremiah," *JBL* 70 (1951): 15-35. The Job traditions are multi-layered and came together through a complex redactional process. For an overview, see Marvin Pope, *Job* (Garden City: Doubleday, 1965). For a recent treatment, see Carol A. Newsom, *The Book of Job: A Contest of Moral Imaginations* (New York: Oxford University Press,

signifies the community as constituted by guilt,[54] and simultaneously signals the same to its members. After the performative drama of public mourning, Ezra finally speaks in verses 6-7. As if the acts of silent lament were insufficient to express the weightiness of "this thing," from verse 3, Ezra reacts verbally to the people's actions, signifying on the intermarriages by noting pointedly "this guilt has risen above our heads."

In Ezra 9:7, the rhetoric makes a temporal shift. It takes up the offense against Yahweh as one in a long sequence of offenses that have occurred throughout ancient Israelite history. With the words, "from the days of our ancestors," the guilt that earlier was local and referred only to the present instance of ethnic intermixing in the contemporaneous, political context of the Persian province of Yehud now becomes transhistorical. The rhetoric connects the *golah* to an ancient metanarrative tradition, claiming, in the next phrase, that from their beginning, as far back as the days of their ancestors, they "have been in great guilt." The past indebts them to Yahweh not only because of the current transgression but also, according to verse 6, for an entire history of iniquities that are so great that they have arisen above their heads and their unfaithfulness has expanded to the heavens. With this final indictment, there is no escape, no release from the immensity of this guilt. It not only comprises the current intermarriage crisis, it also includes generations of offenses over which this contemporary community had no control and of which they probably were not even aware. The fivefold expression of culpability[55] undermines any moral standing. For them, the rhetoric programs the proper response to this indictment; they can only tremble (v. 4) in fear at the seriousness of this charge.

In 9:7b, the rhetorical strategy shifts from indictment to judgment. Rendering the judgment imposed by Yahweh, Ezra reveals to

---

2003). For the context of Job in Persian Yehud, see Berquist, *Judaism in Persia's Shadow*, 208.

[54] The symbolic acts connect this sign of guilt to ancient traditions giving the community a historical reference that finds meaning in the prophetic and wisdom traditions.

[55] Guilt (9:6), great guilt (9:7), iniquity (9:6, 9:7), and unfaithfulness (9:4).

the congregation a judgment that ostensibly includes the entire community, "we," "our kings," and "our priests" "have been given into the hands of the kings of the lands."[56] Using four short prepositional phrases that each act as an adverb, the rhetoric voices the state of the people's lives under imperial domination: Yahweh has given them over "to the sword," "to captivity," "to spoil," and "to utter shame." Finally, verse 7 closes with the phrase, "to this day," the *terminus ad quem* for the phrase opening the verse, "From the days of our ancestors." This last phrase reiterates the temporal parameters of this pervasive guilt; it encompasses their entire existence from their beginning until the present.

In Ezra 9:8-9a the rhetorical strategy progresses, moving from judgment to acceptance. The acceptance motif recasts the state of domination. At the same time it communicates the people's expected role in the imperial system. Having made the judgment explicit in the phrases, "to the sword, to captivity, to spoil, and to utter shame" (9:7b), the rhetoric refers instead to the Persian land-grant, most likely the land tenured to the Second Temple temple and that controlled by other members of the aristocracy.[57] It recasts the community's subjugated political status as a form of Yahweh's favor (9:8). That favor is tenure to land (which the rhetoric identifies as "a stake [*lit. tent peg*] in this holy place") in this western frontier of the empire. In this instance, the rhetoric even intends that the *golah* should gladly accept their lot, stating that by giving them this "stake," Yahweh has "lightened our eyes and given to us a little sustenance" (9:8). Their imperative is to comply with the Persian program of agricultural intensification by producing the

---

[56] J. Meyers argues this phrase refers to the kings of Persia. Jacob Meyers, *Ezra Nehemiah* (ed. William Foxwell Albright and David Noel Freedman; New York: Doubleday, 1965), 75. He cites A. T. Clay, *Business Documents of Murashû* (vol. 2 part 1; Philadelphia: University of Pennsylvania, 1912), 28 n. 6. The first common plural speaks from the perspective of an in-group who identify themselves as "true Israel" and who legitimate their economic and political claims with that understanding (Becking, "We All Returned as One!" 3-18).

[57] Hoglund, *Achaemenid*, 238. M. A. Dandamaev, "The Domain-Lands of Achaemenes in Babylonia," *AoF* 1(1974): 123-27.

agricultural surplus needed by the imperial bureaucracy.[58] Verse 8 closes, and verse 9 begins by acknowledging the state of domination under which the *golah* live as an enslaved people ("in our enslavement" in 9:8, and "for we are slaves" in 9:9) to Persia. In the latter portion of the verse, 9:9b, the rhetoric again shifts to the task before the *golah*. Yahweh's favor has given them the opportunity to rebuild the temple. By the end of verses 8 and 9, the political intentionality of the rhetoric is clear. It encourages the people not to *challenge* their political status, but rather to *accept culpability* for it and then to participate in the Persian program of ruralization by taking a "stake in this holy place," and by supporting the temple, in order "to raise up the house of our God."

In its political signification, the rhetoric's strategy is threefold. It constructs the community as guilty of an egregious offense against Yahweh and levies against them a fivefold indictment (Ezra 9:3-7a). Laden with guilt so overwhelming that it has "risen above their heads and expanded to the heavens," the community no longer has any moral ground on which to stand. It cannot complain, for as Ezra cries out in 9:6, "I am too ashamed and humiliated to lift my face to you, God...." It has no choice but to "tremble" (9:4) in fear, and to accept the judgment of Yahweh. The judgment in 9:7b is divinely-ordained imperial domination, for Yahweh had given them "into the hands of the kings of the land, to the sword, to captivity, to plunder, and to utter shame." The declaration grounds imperial rule in divine legitimation. To question the priestly rhetoric or to rebel against imperial authority is to rebel against Yahweh. Finally, in 9:8-9, the third stratagem moves the rhetoric from judgment to acceptance, encouraging the *golah* to accept their "enslavement" and to support the temple.

Conclusion

Beginning with the conquest of the Neo-Babylonian Empire, the Persians conscripted local temples and their respective priesthoods toward fulfilling imperial priorities. These priorities included maintaining internal stability, encouraging loyalty among local populations, and facilitating the orderly flow of tributes for imperial use.

---

[58] See chapter 8 of Lenski, *Power and Privilege*. This task is essential for agrarian societies.

Generally, Persian authorities coerced local temple officials to comply with imperial interests by threatening violence and dispossession or persuading them to cooperate with patronage, which included increased wealth or status.

In return for imperial favor or to forestall imperial repression, local priesthoods produced pro-imperial propaganda to present Persian rule as a legitimate succession to the previous order. In Babylon, Cyrus compelled the disaffected priesthood of Marduk, whom Nabonidus had alienated, to present his rule as a restoration of Babylonian tradition. In the Cyrus Cylinder and the Verse Account of Nabonidus, they portray Cyrus as Marduk's emissary, a divinely commissioned envoy, whom Marduk raised up as the legitimate ruler. In Egypt, Udjahorresnet capitulates to the Persians and is named Chief Physician at the House of Life, the Sanctuary of Neith at Sais. It is a highly visible position, but one with little real political power. Cambyses and Darius I both patronize the temple granting tenure to arable land and removing occupying soldiers. In return, Udjahorresnet constructs titles for the Achaemenid king that present their rule as legitimate extensions of the 26th dynasty. Similar to their counterparts in Babylon and Egypt, the Second Temple priesthood in Jerusalem negotiated the imperial system. Their literature communicates a sovereign narrative just as did their counterparts throughout the empire. In three rhetorical moves, Ezra 9 assures the empire of its sovereignty and engrafts the community's efforts, loyalties, and identity into the imperial system.

Chapter 4

Countering the Imperial Story: Subversive Voice and Cultic Significations

Subverting the Imperial Will

The rhetoric's dominant language articulates a narrative of the sovereign, the Persian Empire, that rules with a progressive beneficence and a *laissez faire* imperative. It is the story of uninterrupted Persian hegemony across the field of system of undifferentiated fealty from local communities throughout the imperial system. However, this narrative exists in dialectic with an alternative, namely a counter-history.

Contrary to long-standing arguments characterizing the local Persian administration as *laissez faire,* we now know that the Persians invested heavily in an extensive bureaucracy with checks and balances that imposed the imperial will at every level. Because temple complexes were centers for the political, judicial, and economic life of their locales, each level of the Persian bureaucracy directed some part of their operation.[1] The empire's administrative presence left little room for temples to resist imperial will. Temples had a profound influence over the prevailing ideology of their adherents, so regulating them was essential for the successful administration of the satrapy. In Babylon and

---

[1] For a discussion of temple complexes as the central organizing and unifying institution in ancient Near Eastern societies, see John M. Lundquist, "What Is a Temple? A Preliminary Typology," in *The Quest for the Kingdom of God: Studies in Honor of George E. Mendenhall* (ed. H. B. Huffmon, et al.; Winona Lake, Ind.: Eisenbrauns, 1983), 205-19.

Egypt, temple complexes and imperial authorities existed in tension rather than worked in tandem. On the one hand, the monarchy sought to control the priesthood without losing popular support. The priesthood, on the other hand, often resorted to appropriating divine authority to retain as much autonomy as possible.[2] The cultic signification of Ezra 9-10 reflects the Second Temple community's resistance to the imperial system.

Military Apparatus and Temple Resistance

On occasion where episodes of such local resistance tested the imperial will, the empire responded with strategic displays of public violence. These were effective reminders for temples of the scope of imperial power, and took many forms. In Egypt, the Persians wrested the well-trained Egyptian warrior class from the employ of powerful temple complexes and placed them under commanders of Persian ethnicity.[3] In Babylonia, Xerxes reportedly destroyed temples that fomented rebellion

---

[2] Kautsky, *The Politics of Aristocratic Empires*, 251. Kautsky argues that except where the ruler was head of the religious organization, "priestly powers were derived from a source other than the ruler."

[3] For temples, there was often little distinction between military and political figures. Persian officials used military appointments as opportunities to move up in the governing bureaucracy, even crossing from military to political administration. An Elephantine papyrus records an interesting account of the career of the Persian official, Waidrang, and thus, some insight into the Persian military structure. In a papyrus dated to 420 B.C.E., he is mentioned as a Troop Commander [*haftaopata*]. He is Guardian of the Seven by 416 B.C.E., then *fratarak* by 410 B.C.E. Bezalel Porten, *The Elephantine Papyri in English: Three Millennia of Cross-Cultural Continuity and Change*, (Documenta et monumenta Orientis antiqui (DMOA), Studies in Near Eastern archaeology and civilisation 22; Atlanta: Society of Biblical Literature, 2012), B15, B31, and B42. In B32 he is also a troop commander, not simply a chief. There must also have been lesser commanders since the garrisons are also subdivided into *degelin*. Each *degel* bore the name of its commander. The names are generally Persian. All were under the command of the *rab haila* at Syene. Bezalel Porten and Ada Yardeni, *Textbook of Aramaic Documents from Ancient Egypt* (4 vols.; Winona Lake, In, U.S.A.: Eisenbrauns, 1986), A4.7.

by fostering nationalistic sentiments.[4] In Egypt, an Aramaic papyrus from the military colony at Elephantine reports Cambyses's mass destruction of Egyptian sanctuaries. The papyrus seeks to elevate the status of the *Yahu* temple at Elephantine over other cults,

> "And from the days of the king(s) of Egypt our fathers had built that temple in the Elephantine fortress, and when Cambyses entered Egypt, that temple built he found it. And the temples of the gods of Egypt (all of them), they overthrew, but anything in that temple one did not damage."[5]

Herodotus reports the public slaughter of 2,000 young Egyptian males by Cambyses.[6] There are also reports of the Persian use of force against Egyptian priests.[7] Military force, however, was expensive. It required huge armies whose soldiers had to be paid, oftentimes with land grants or in-kind compensation in the form of agricultural produce. Despite imperial repression, temples resisted as much as was feasible without inciting violent retribution.

---

[4] Xerxes destroyed local temples after the revolt in Babylon. Olmstead, *A History of the Persian Empire*, 236-37. Olmstead relies on Ctesias *Persica* xiii.b who locates the destruction before the campaign against the Greeks. However, Diodorus II.9.4ff and Strabo XVI.1.5 locate the destruction after the Greek campaign. With regard to the veracity of the account and anti-Persian bias in the Greek sources, see Amélie Kuhrt and Susan Sherwin-White, "Xerxes' Destruction of Babylonian Temples," in *Achaemenid History II: The Greek Sources* (ed. Heleen Sancisi-Weerdenburg and Amélie Kuhrt; Leiden: Nederlands Instituut Voor Het Nabije Oosten, 1987), 70. The historicity of this specific account is less important than the imperial power to which it attests.

[5] Porten, *The Elephantine Papyri*, B19.

[6] Herodotus, *The History,* III.14 (Greene).

[7] Herodotus, *The History,* III.29 (Greene). The facts of this story, which primarily concern Cambyses's murder of the Apis Bull, are inconclusive. More than likely Cambyses did not kill the Apis bull. An epitaph dating to 524 B.C.E. discovered at the Serapeum of Memphis where the Apises were interred states that the Apis was buried with full funerary rites and the participation of the Pharaoh. Yet, stories of Cambyses's public displays of violence abound.

Political Apparatus and Temple Resistance

Immediately after conquering Babylonia and Egypt, Persian kings appointed a satrap[8] or governor, whose duty it was to execute the orders given by the central authority.[9] The office carried out day-to-day administrative duties in the territory. Its power extended throughout the political, judicial, military, and cultic realms of the society.[10] In the absence of the native monarch this meant directly engaging temple complexes. The satrap, who for all practical purposes ruled the territory,

---

[8] The use of this term is somewhat confusing. The primary sources use various terms for the supreme imperial authority located in the conquered territories. A Gu-bar-u' and later Uštanu both recognized as satraps of Babylonia (535 B.C.E.) and Ebr-Nahara, are actually given the Aramaic title "governor." Aryandes, whom Cambyses leaves in charge of Egypt, is given the more general title *hyparkhos*. Herodotus, *The History*. IV.166 (Greene). In Egypt, however, we find the demotic rendering of satrap, *hštrpn*. Scholars have identified each of these figures with the term *satrap*, presumably for the sake of convenience. Gradually, during Darius's reign, Old Iranian administrative and legal terms began to appear in Babylonian documents. From three of the Murashu Documents of Nippur during the latter part of the fifth century B.C.E., we see the word *ahšad(a)rapannu* which is the Babylonian transcription of the Old Persian world *xšaçapavan* (literally, guardian of the kingdom). M. A. Dandamaev, *Iranians in Achaemenid Babylonia* (ed. Ehsan Yarshater; vol. 6; New York: Mazda Publishers, 1992), 5. However, this does not mean that the office of satrap was a convention of Darius's reign, but his reign gives rise to greater use of the term.

[9] Cambyses's rule ends in 525 B.C.E., the same year he conquers Egypt. Before he dies however, he leaves Aryandes in place as satrap. Herodotus, *The History,* IV.166 (Greene). By 535 B.C.E., Gubaru served as satrap of Babylonia under Cyrus and Cambyses. Briant, *From Cyrus to Alexander*, 64.

[10] Although the satraps wielded vast power, the king kept a close watch and removed satraps at will. A chronology of the satrapy of Egypt is an interesting case. Aryandes ruled as satrap under Cambyses from the Persian conquest to 522 B.C.E., the year of Cambyses's death and Darius's ascension to the throne. He is executed when Darius returns to Egypt in 519 B.C.E. presumably for an attempt to establish his rule over Egypt. Herodotus, *The History,* IV.166 (Greene).

functioned directly under the Persian king. In the provinces, the satrap was the visible representation of the king's will and authority. Often satraps emphasized their governing power by residing in the palaces confiscated from former kings. For the empire, this practice served multiple purposes. First, it reinforced the satrap's presence as supplanting that of the former monarch. Second, the residences were large enough to serve as bureaucratic centers and as depositories for official government documents. The palaces also served as residences for the king during imperial visits. The Persians seized royal residences in Ecbatana, Sardi, Bactra, Babylon, Susa, Saïs, and Memphis.[11]

Among a satrap's basic responsibilities were to establish tributes (as the next chapter shows, temples become increasingly important in fiscal matters) to Susa and to place imperial garrisons at strategic locales throughout the newly conquered territory. At his disposal, the satrap had a local contingent of the royal army to provide support by intimidating local populations with its mere presence.[12] Because the satrap wielded an enormous amount of power, the king trusted the office to only a member of the royal family or to a prominent but loyal Persian aristocrat.[13]

Below the office of the satrap, Persians installed a complex bureaucracy to oversee the administrative provinces in the vast territories of the satrapy of Egypt, and the satrapy of Babylonia and Ebr-Nahara. Each level of the Persian bureaucracy strengthened the crown's

---

[11] Herodotus, *The History*. I.98, (David Greene, The estates of Parysatis are attested in Xenophon. Xenophon, *Anabasis*. II.4.27 and I.4.9-10, (Carleton L. Brownson, LCL). Queen Paysatis's vast land ownership is attested in several Babylonian documents. M. A. Dandamaev et al., *The Culture and Social Institutions of Ancient Iran* (Cambridge; New York: Cambridge University Press, 1989), 136.

[12] This power sometimes proved to be a danger to the central authority as in the case of Oroetes, satrap of Sardis. Herodotus, *The History,* III.127 (Greene).

[13] In Egypt: Aryandes (522–519). Herodotus, *The History,* IV.166 (Greene); Pherendates (519–492) PBerlin 13539, 13540; Achaemenes (485–?) Herodotus, *The History,* VII.7 (Greene). In Babylonia: Gubāru (535-525), Uštānu (521-516). For ethnic identification, see M.A. Dandamaev, *Iranians in Achaemenid*. See also Briant, *From Cyrus to Alexander*, 82, 351-2.

administrative hold on the provinces. Egyptian provinces were governed by a *fratara-ka-*.[14] In Babylonia, a Persian with the Babylonian title, *paq-du* held similar responsibilities.[15] Chief administrators of cities were generally given the title *šaknu te'em* (Chief of the Order).[16] Subordinate to the provincial managers were city governors or governors of smaller regions. In Xenophon's *Anabasis*, there is a Belesys identified as ruler of Syria who may have been a provincial governor at Babylon and then governor of Across-the-River between 421–401.[17] The Persians used two other titles for city governors. The first, *u-mar-za-na-pa-ta*, the Babylonian transcription of the Old Persian *vardana pāti*, Dandamaev translates as "chief of the city."[18] The second is an *up-pa-de-tu* attested in a document from 523 B.C.E., as early as the reign of Cambyses, recording the sale of two enslaved persons before the official Umar'mina who was *up-pa-de-tu* of Hamadesu in the region of Persepolis.[19]

Both judicial and political authority often resided in the same officials. As soon as it was feasible to do so, the Persians dispensed with the old, popular Babylonian city assemblies (which provided for a more democratized judicial system) that competed with the royal court for judicial authority. This new policy relegated the Old Babylonian city assembly to adjudicating small property disputes and minor civil

---

[14] Porten, *The Elephantine Papyri*, B31. Tavernier 4.4.7.42

[15] Dandamaev, *Iranians in Achaemenid Babylonia*, 5.

[16] Complicating the matter, the Persians used these titles, *šaknu* and satrap, for various other levels of administration. Ibid., 5-6. The title *šaknu* referred to Assyrian officials in the Babylonian period also designated an overseer of professional, military, and ethnic groups and governors of the city of Nippur. Matthew W. Stolper, "The *šaknu of Nuppur*," *JCS* 40 (1988): 127-55.

[17] Matthew W. Stolper, "Belšunu the Satrap," in *Language, Literature and History: Philological and Historical Studies Presented to Erica Reiner* (ed. F. Rochberg-Halton; AOS 67; New Haven: American Oriental Society 1987), 392. Xenophon, *Anabasis*. I.4.10.

[18] Tavenier 4.4.7.130. See also Briant, *From Cyrus to Alexander,* 485. See also Dandamaev, *Iranians in Achaemenid Babylonia*, 6-7.

[19] Briant, *From Cyrus*, 7. See also Tavernier 4.4.7.109

offenses.[20] Under the Persians, judicial administration belonged to the administrative realm of the imperial rather than native authorities. Any legal matters that affected the maintenance of order or the collection of tribute came directly under the purview of the satrap or a lower Persian official. Babylonian aristocrats thus had to appeal to a satrap for criminal petitions.[21] As Persian interest in judicial affairs increased, the crown dispatched judges of Persian ethnicity to Babylonia as early as the reign of Darius I.[22] There is evidence that he added an official to the judicial apparatus, a *mvitiprasu*, an interrogator,[23] who worked in tandem with the Persian judge as an "investigator of the court," ensuring that the judge had all needed facts in order to protect Persian interests. In Egypt, the Persians created a dual system of legal administration, one for natives, and one for foreigners. Aside from the satrap, there was a "lord of the command," who administered legal affairs for the satrap. In various Aramaic documents, a host of other officials appear. King's judges administered justice at the satrapal level; their counterparts, constables (*tī-pati)*,[24] operated at the provincial level; and the *gausaka* researched for the king.[25]

In this bureaucratic milieu, we begin to understand that temples faced constant imperial intervention in their routine affairs. The crown's adminstrative innovations only reinforced the work of the imperial bureaucracy. For example, Darius I's reputation as lawgiver and the sixth and last legislator of Egypt[26] connects imperial administration to local

---

[20] Dandamaev, *Iranians in Achaemenid Babylonia*, 9.

[21] Stolper, *Entrepreneurs and Empire: The Murasu Archive, the Murasu Firm, and Persian Rule in Babylonia*, 94. See also EEMA 109.

[22] Dandamaev, *Iranians in Achaemenid Babylonia*, 9.

[23] See G. J. P. McEwan, *The Late Babylonian Tablets in the Royal Ontario Museum* (vol. 2; Toronto: 1982). See McEwan's translation in 2:36.

[24] Tavernier 4.4.7.106.

[25] Xenophon, *Cyropaedia.* VIII.2.10 (Walter Miller, LCL). See also Tavernier 4.4.7.53.

[26] Diodorus, *Library of History,* 1.94–95 (Oldfather, LCL.) While the account itself is disputed, it demonstrates the Persian king's authority over temple laws. An example in the next section shows Darius's use of his legislative power.

temples. A Demotic papyrus claims that in the third year of Darius's reign, he instructed the satrap to assemble the "wisemen," soldiers, priests, and scribes of Egypt to codify the Egyptian legal system from the last year of Amasis's Rule, 526 B.C.E.[27] Working for sixteen years (519–503), the commission produced a legal compendium in three categories, "temple law," "official law," and "common or civil law." Although not much is known about the content of this compendium of laws, it was produced in both Demotic, the administrative language of Egyptian elites, and Aramaic, the administrative language of Persia. The Aramaic translation shrewdly gave the mostly Persian imperial officials the ability to be much more closely involved in temple affairs. Once Darius was familiar with temple law, and, of course, had played a major role in its legislation and enforcement, he could dictate the affairs of temples more effectively. Since native elites also participated in creating the compendium, they were invested in maintaining its legitimacy.

Despite or perhaps because of Darius's legislative authority, Egypt's temple complexes resisted Persia's direct interference in their affairs. An incident described in two Demotic letters shows an Egyptian wab-priest at the temple of Khnum violating Persian law regarding the eligibility of persons to serve as temple officials. The first letter dated April 21, 492 B.C.E., written by Pharandates, satrap of Egypt, concerns the appointment of a *lesonis*.[28] In it, Pharandates admonishes the *wab*-priest that the men previously brought before him to be appointed *lesonis* did not meet the criteria set out by Darius.[29] He reiterates those criteria and instructs the priest to send a suitable candidate. One of the criteria is

---

[27] W. Spiegelberg, *Die sogenannte demotische Chronik des Pap. 215 der Bibliothèque Nationale zu Paris* (Leipzig: 1914), column C, 6-16, in Amélie Kuhrt, *The Persian Empire: A Corpus of Sources from the Achaemenid Period* (2 vols.; vol. 2; London; New York: Routledge, 2007), 125.

[28] Martin identifies the lesonis as "an important temple functionary whose responsibilities lay primarily in administration and organization who was appointed or reappointed annually." Cary J. Martin, "The Demotic Texts," in *The Elephantine Papyri In English: Three Millennia of Cross-Cultural Continuity and Change* (ed. Belazel Porten; New York: E.J. Brill, 1996), 291. n. 6.

[29] Martin, "The Demotic Texts," C1.

of particular interest here: The text states that the *lesonis* may not be the servant of another man. Belazel Porten thinks this stipulation has to do with contractual obligations in terms of debt owed.[30] Clearly, Darius wanted this important temple administrator to have no other legal, financial, or political entanglements that might conflict with the appointee's loyalty to the Persian king.[31] To ensure loyalty, imperial officials evaluated and reappointed the *lesonis* annually. In this case, the wab-priests had attempted to resist imperial intervention in its affairs by disregarding Darius's will. They, of course, prefered a candidate with native loyalties and obligations rather than one whose loyalties lay with the empire.

Darius's power over local cults did not go unchallenged. An episode concerning the priesthood at the temple in Memphis illustrates the limits of imperial control and its encounter with priestly resistance. Although the temple at Memphis had received favorable treatment by Cambyses, in that he did not diminish its funding, the priesthood there did not allow Darius to place his statue above the image of Sesotris.[32] The high priest argued that Darius's accomplishments had not surpassed Sesotris's. Though Diodorus comments that the episode highlights Darius's respect for local religious customs, I suggest that instead this incident shows that Darius's relationship with the priesthood was tenuous and best characterized as a "give and take": Darius asserted as much control as possible without alienating an institution whose support he needed, while the priesthood conceded only what autonomy it was forced to relinquish to imperial authorities. Ultimately, Persia maintained an active presence in governing judicial affairs. As with the political administration, the Persian cadre of officials intervened in strategic places, particularly where judicial affairs related to fiscal matters. In

---

[30] Martin, "The Demotic Texts," 291 n. 8. However, K. Th. Zauzich interprets this condition to mean one who may serve or have allegiance to a political opponent of the satrap in "Die demotischen Papyri von der Insel Elephantine," (1983). Cited here from Martin.

[31] In this instance, Darius is more than a legislator; he effectively becomes a cultic administrator who appoints personnel in the Egyptian temple system.

[32] Diodorus, *Library of History,* IV.54–55 (Oldfather, LCL).

Jerusalem, resistance took the form of rhetoric and ritual by which the priesthood reimagined its relationship to the community and the empire.

Analyzing the Rhetoric:
Subverting Dominion and Legitimating the Priesthood

Prima facie, the rhetoric of Ezra 9-10 has a cultic-theological orientation. It deploys symbolic acts, a concern for purity, law, the house of God, and the roles of religious functionaries. These symbols find their significance in the power of the deity rather than the political authorities. The Second Temple priesthood was keenly aware that its legitimacy had to come from Yahweh, not the empire, in order to be effective in negotiating the imperial system. In a context where the cult is virtually "planted" by the empire's construction of the temple, the priesthood must work to create the structures for divine legitimation over imperial legitimation. The authorities of the First Temple found divine legitimation in the ancient traditions narrating Yahweh's choice of Solomon, son of David, as its architect. The union of civil authority with divine legitimacy that came through stories of Yahweh's covenant with David undergirded the Solomonic temple's cultic activity and promised its priesthood's perpetuation. In the aftermath of the First Temple's destruction and the tragic and humiliating end of the Davidic monarchy, both royal and priestly ideologies suffered a crisis of legitimation. The personnel of this Second Temple priesthood had to repair that crisis and reestablish its own legitimacy. Appropriating symbolic resources, temple officials re-imagined their social world in a manner that supported the priesthood's authority. Without this legitimation, the Second Temple and its priesthood existed merely as a creation of the empire.[33] To vest the Second Temple priesthood with divine legitimation, the rhetoric's counter knowledge dissociates the cult's establishment from the activity

---

[33] Rainer Albertz states the problem plainly, "[T]he post-exilic Jerusalem cult was still a state cult in so far as the Persian king had contributed part of the building costs (Ezra 6.4), and also continued to make contributions to support the regular sacrificial cult (6.8-10;7.21-23). In return, the foreign [that is, Persian] authorities asked for sacrifices and intercessions for the life of the royal family and for the ongoing existence of the empire. (6.10; 7.23)." Rainer Albertz, *A History of Israelite Religion in the Old Testament Period* (Louisville, Ky: Westminster John Knox, 1994), 459.

of Persians and connects it with the power, the authority, and the will of Yahweh.

The rhetoric's coded and explicit connections between the Second Temple and Solomon's temple establish the authority of the contemporary priesthood—now undergirded by Persian beneficence—by associating it with the ancient priesthood of Aaron and Levi. It constructs the identity of *golah*, who are a people deported by the Persians to develop a desolate western frontier of the empire, by alluding to fictive genealogies (the *bet 'abot*), and connects them to the ancient *toledoth* of an earlier era. The rhetoric deploys two strategies to ground the cult with divine legitimation. The first strategy employs symbolic acts in a ritualized fashion. The second strategy appropriates Israelite history, its symbols, personages, and traditions to connect the Second Temple community to pre-exilic Israel surveying Canaan from the Transjordan. Finally, the rhetoric appropriates power. In this cultic sense, power enforces the will of temple authorities. It threatens the community's destruction by Yahweh and by other members of the temple community as a just consequence of disobedience. In these ways, the Second Temple priesthood establishes its authority within the community.

Resistance, Rhetoric, Performance, and Ritual Space

In its cultic signification, the rhetoric takes the form of a religious ritual, deploying the symbols of the people's cultural history to construct an Israelite identity for those now living in Jerusalem. This Israelite identity emphasizes three theological ideas: that the power of Yahweh trumps Persian domination; that the Second Temple is the symbol of Yahweh's presence rather than an instrument of the Persian bureaucratic apparatus; and that the Jerusalem priests are emissaries of Yahweh rather than local agents of the empire.

With cultic ritual performance,[34] the Second Temple priesthood carves out a sacred space and sacred time ordered by their own

---

[34] Frank Gorman argues that this is precisely the proper method for the study of ritual, arguing that any study of ritual must begin with the "recognition that ritual is a socio-cultural act which takes place in a specific socio-cultural context" (*The Ideology of Ritual: Space, Time, and Status in the Priestly Theology* [ed. David J. A. Clines; Sheffield: Sheffield Academic Press, 1990], 14). In this instance, the ritual must be understood as a process that has arisen

worldview,[35] a worldview that trumps that of the imperial authorities. The priesthood deploys religious myths whose sacred symbols legitimate institutions and forms of consciousness, imbuing current social realities with cosmic meaning. Using rituals, they enact and (re)enact these myths, kinesthetically encouraging the acceptance of certain values. Such myths affirm the interests, institutions, and power of one segment of a society, in this case, Second Temple priesthood.[36] Within this ritual space, the rhetoric counters imperial legitimation of the temple by imbuing the temple and its priesthood with divine legitimation in order to construct a counter-identity for the community.

By extension, ritual performance in Ezra 9–10 also has both a moral and a communicative dimension. From the perspective of the priesthood, the ritual brings together in a sacred space the world as it is and the world as the priesthood desires it to be. The ritual communicates

---

out of necessity from a particular social context— imperial domination—and has meaning in that same material matrix. For a foundational discussion on the function of religious ritual in the social world, see Emile Durkheim, *Elementary Forms of Religious Life* (trans. Karen Elise Fields; New York: Free Press, 1995). See also Yonina Dor who gives a well-argued discussion for reading Ezra 9:1-10:1 as ritual. While I agree that the rhetoric represents ritual performance, I disagree with the position that ritual was the *sole* action to address the community's real distress, which I will present in chapter 5. Yonina Dor, "The Rite of Separation of the Foreign Wives in Ezra-Nehemiah," in *Judah and Judeans in the Achaemenid Period* (ed. Oded Lipschits, Gary N. Knoppers, and Manfred Oeming; Winona Lake, In.: Eisenbrauns, 2011).

[35] Mircea Eliade, *The Sacred and the Profane: The Nature of Religion* (trans. Willard R. Trask; New York: Harcourt Brace Jovanovich, 1987), 20-29.

[36] Myths provide cosmic legitimation for institutions and belief systems, rooting the social reality in cosmic origins. Ritual shows the relationships embodied by institutions, and rituals encourage the popular acceptance of such myths. In this interpretation of myth and ritual, it is not surprising to find a coercive aspect to ritual. If rituals create assent to myths through an action that embodies a mythic support for an institution, then rituals coerce the acceptance of ideologies of the status quo or of some power group's desires for reality. See Berquist, *Judaism in Persia's Shadow*, 148-49.

both worlds to its audience using symbolic forms.[37] In this way, sacred rituals conveys the priesthood's values, norms, and beliefs about the world, its order, and its relationship to the deity. Through the rhetoric, the ritual system holds a definite idea about the created order, which includes both the natural order and the societal order. In the performance, the Second Temple priesthood participates in maintaining divine order (the world as the priesthood desires it to be) against imperial rule (the world as it is).

As a regulative mechanism, the ritual therefore orders the processes, functions, and webs of relations within the Second Temple community. This function of ritual works in two ways: it stabilizes a particular sociocultural system, and it restores a sociocultural order that has been ruptured.[38] For the Second Temple community, Ezra 9 associates the temple with older cultural symbols and legitimates its conception as an extension of Yahweh's power. This association also disrupts the temple's conception as a creation of the Persian Empire. In so doing, the ritual as a morally prescriptive and performative act[39] maintains certain cultural boundaries and restores (to right order) boundaries no longer intact.

With these explanations in mind, we can now turn to Ezra's activities in chapters 9–10 as they act out a ritualized drama, a drama in which Ezra performs specific "symbolic acts" designed to communicate the rupture in the relationship between Yahweh and the *golah*. In the social world, this rupture is Persian control of the temple and the intermixing of the *golah*. In the symbolic universe of cultic signs, the ritual attempts to restore that order. Its form comprises four symbolic acts and five speeches alternately directed to Yahweh and to the *golah*.

---

[37] Clifford Geertz, *The Interpretation of Cultures* (New York: Basic Books, 1973), 12.

[38] Gorman, *The Ideology of Ritual* 29.

[39] For the idea of ritual as performance, see Victor Turner, *From Ritual to Theatre: The Human Seriousness of Play* (New York: Performing Arts Journal Publications, 1982, 1982), 61-88.

Ezra's symbolic acts fit within the ritual category of status. In each symbolic act, Ezra mediates between two ritual statuses.[40] In his role as priest, Ezra mediates between the (divine) status of the holy/pure and the people's status through intermarriage as not-holy/impure. Simultaneously, Ezra's speeches alternate between symbolic spaces in which he holds an audience with Yahweh and those in which subsequently he holds an audience with the *golah*. After finally leading the people to the temple, the rhetoric concludes the speeches directed to Yahweh, and instead Ezra and Shecaniah's rhetoric at the temple leads the people to begin the process of dissolving the intermarriages.

Ezra 9:1-2 opens by disclosing this breach in the cosmic order that intermarriage symbolizes. For the priesthood, the problem is the permeation of status boundaries. In 9:3, Ezra performs the first of four symbolic acts, designed to communicate to the Second Temple community the state of the cosmic order and to repair that order by changing the behavior of the *golah*. Upon hearing the report of the mixed marriages, he rends his garment and his cloak, pulls hair from his head and beard, and sits in desolation. In these symbolic acts, Ezra signifies his lament for the guilt of the community. By disheveling his appearance and by acts of self-mutilation, Ezra takes on the representation of the breach in the cosmic order and communicates this to the people. Blenkinsopp sees Ezra's actions as "what we would today call the P.R. angle for, as Josephus notes (*Ant.* 11.142), these demonstrative acts had the advantage of drawing public attention to his protest."[41] In the next verse, the rhetoric programs the proper response of the populace in acknowledgment of this breach. They all tremble at the "word of the God of Israel."

In dramatic fashion, in 9:5-6, Ezra's symbolic acts signal a status shift from his audience with the people to an audience with Yahweh,

---

[40] This concern for status reflects the priestly understanding that order emerges through the correct separation of categories and the maintenance of boundaries. The priests are told to separate between the holy and the not-holy, between the clean and the unclean. In a worldview so concerned with category distinction, it is not surprising that a major concern of ritual focuses on the issue of status. Gorman, *The Ideology of Ritual*, 59.

[41] Blenkinsopp, *Ezra-Nehemiah*, 177.

from the "not-holy" to the "holy." The rhetoric describes his actions in terms of a public performative drama. Ezra arises from his self-abasement with his garments torn, he bows down upon his knees, spreads his hands to Yahweh, and finally, having completed the transition in ritual status, he speaks, confessing his utter shame and humiliation to Yahweh.

After Ezra's audience with Yahweh in 9:5-6, his rhetoric shifts the ritual space once again, this time from "holy" to "not-holy," from Yahweh to the *golah*. He instructs them as to the nature of their guilt and the consequence of the breach. They must live under the kings of the lands as enslaved persons. Made clear through a system of signs that comprise the community's cultural history, the nature of this domination in the rhetoric's cultic signification counters its political signification, its dominant language. In the political signification, Persian authorities hear affirmation of the imperial system. The cultic signification counters imperial authority. It is not the power of the empire that dominates the *golah;* rather, in the sacred space of the ritual, Yahweh's power is sovereign. It is the power of Yahweh that has *given* them (9:7) into the hands of the kings of the lands. So the dominion of the empire (the world as it is) is supplanted by the sovereignty of Yahweh (the world as it should be). The rhetoric brings the two together in the world of ritual. For the temple community, verses 7-9 reinforce Yahweh's power over the community. More important, in this symbolic universe Yahweh's power over the empire, which the priesthood mediates, also trumps the empire's power over the temple community.

In Ezra 9:10-11, the status of the ritual alternates a third time. Ezra returns again to an audience with Yahweh. In this speech, Ezra poses a question to Yahweh as to how the community might repair this breach in the cosmic order. In verse 12, the fourth shift, the rhetoric returns to an audience with the people, in which Ezra relates Yahweh's instructions against them intermarrying with the people of the land, such abstinence being capable of repairing the breach in the cosmic order.

In verses 13-15, Ezra again turns from the community and returns to an audience with Yahweh. The rhetoric's fifth shift focuses on power. It legitimates the ability of the cult to mediate the power of the God. Verse 14 shows the nature of this power: Yahweh will "finish off" the *golah* "without even a remnant or a survivor." Only through the people's obedience will Yahweh continue to hold back just punishment for their disruption of the cosmic order.

In Ezra 10:1 the rhetoric's final spatial shift places Ezra "before the house of God," praying and confessing before Yahweh. There the people join him. Ezra no longer moves between audiences with Yahweh and the people, the realms of the "holy" and "not-holy;" now, he and the people together petition Yahweh before the house of God. At the temple, the rhetoric resolves this spatial rupture, bringing together the realms of the "holy" and "not-holy," occupied by Yahweh and the people, respectively. Once the rhetoric brings the ritual to Ezra at the temple, it no longer shifts between the spatial realms of Yahweh and the *golah*. Through the remainder of chapter 10, the ritual no longer addresses Yahweh. The temple has become a permanent sacred space, bridging the two realms, mediating between Yahweh and the *golah;* it is again the central symbol of Yahweh's power. Here, both Ezra the priest and the community can gather before the deity. Just as the literature identifies the status of the temple with the state of the Second Temple community, repairing the temple or "raising it from its ruins" metaphorically alludes to repairing the crisis of legitimation for the cult and the temple community. At the temple, the breach is repaired and the relationship between the Second Temple community and Yahweh is reestablished.

After legitimation, the rhetoric attends to priestly authority; it has resolved the breach in the cosmic order at the temple and turns to resolve the breach in the social order. It employs certain priestly figures to speak for the populace or to lead them in behaviors that will restore Yahweh's favor. In doing so, it reinforces priestly authority over the community. Ezra 10:1 begins by invoking symbolic acts of public prayer and confession, which it pairs with the image of Ezra throwing himself to the ground before the deity. Invoking the image of the new, imperially constructed temple, the rhetoric brings together two powerful symbols of legitimation for priestly authority in the province, the temple and Yahweh, whose power is mediated by the Second Temple priesthood. In Ezra 10:2, Shecaniah, one of the priests, speaks on behalf of the people, confessing for them and calling them in verse 3 to enter into a covenant to rid the community of foreign wives. In verse 4, Shecaniah speaks again, this time to Ezra. He commends to Ezra the responsibility to carry out the intention of the divorce rhetoric. With cultic authority, Shecaniah assures Ezra of the community's consent, commanding him to begin the work, "Rise up, for the matter is upon you! We are with you. Be strong! Do it!" The rhetorical force of three imperatives reveals by form and content Shecaniah's authority as a priest. In matters of the cult, he commands even Ezra. In his response, the cult also speaks for the people. Although we do not hear the voices of the people's assent to the divorces, the rhetoric intends their silence to be interpreted as assent to priestly authority over them.

By referencing Shecaniah, a priest with a Yahwistic name meaning "Yahweh resides," the rhetoric signals the credibility of his speech. Perhaps Yahweh abides with this priest who saw first the gravity of the problem, the sincerity of Ezra's symbolic acts of lament, and the validity of Ezra's call to separation that restores both cosmos and society to proper divine order. The rhetoric concludes his exhortation with an appeal to divine law and those who revere it. In verses 3-4, Shecaniah becomes a symbol of legitimation for priestly authority. His vocal support of the rhetoric of Ezra's reforms at the temple and his allusion to the law of God bring together the two most powerful symbols of priestly legitimation: the temple over which the priesthood administers and Yahweh, whose power the priesthood mediates. By invoking these two symbols in tandem, the rhetoric counters the idea of the temple as a symbol of imperial legitimation. In the remainder of chapter 10, the temple authorities perform the will of Yahweh. At the temple, Shecaniah leads the people in covenant with Yahweh, and Ezra proceeds to set apart priests (vv. 18-22), Levites (v. 23), singers (v. 24), and the rest of Israel (vv. 25-43). In the sacred world carved out by this ritualistic perfor-mance, the rhetoric vests the priestly authorities with the power to communicate Yahweh's will and to mediate Yahweh's power for the *golah*.

Finally, two threats of punishment attest to the priesthood's power to effect separation. The first is the ban in Ezra 10:8. Susan Niditch argues that this type of ban is a non-war ban where possessions are not destroyed but rather confiscated from the people for the cult.[42] In

---

[42] See Susan Niditch, *War in the Hebrew Bible: A Study in the Ethics of Violence* (New York: Oxford University Press, 1993), 29. In non-war contexts, Lev 27:28 states that anything that a man devotes to God from among his possession—human beings (i.e., enslaved persons), animals, or agricultural holdings—cannot be purchased or redeemed. That which is in these contexts is

this instance, the community must be persuaded by the priesthood to join together to confiscate the property of the rebellious member and be willing to relinquish that property into the hands of the priesthood. Again, Niditch is helpful, "… the ban is also understood as a means of rooting out the cancerous and contagious 'other': that which is unclean because of sin."[43] In this instance the community would have to perceive its interests as intertwined with those of the priesthood so that they believed that the dissenter who threatens priestly authority also threatens their own survival.

As discussed earlier, the second threat of punishment, found in Ezra 9:14, legitimates the priesthood's authority to mediate the power of Yahweh for the community. In Ezra 9:14, the rhetoric promises that the people's disobedience will incite Yahweh's anger "to finish them off" "without a remnant or a survivor." The rhetoric in this phrase makes the consequences abundantly clear: Yahweh will bring destruction upon the entire community; no one will escape. In the aftermath of the devastation of 587 B.C.E., this threat was real to both the struggling priesthood and the community.

Appropriating the Past to Construct the Present

The second strategy in this cultic signification appropriates the symbols, personalities, and traditions of ancient Israelite history to connect the contemporary postexilic cult with the cult of the Solomonic Temple. The rhetoric frames the temporal perspective of the hearer in two ways. First, it places the *golah* in the distant past, and conceives of them as ancient Israel on the verge of invading Canaan. Second, it places the *golah* in the present, and uses allusions to historical traditions of ancient Israel to connect them to an "ancestry" with particular obligations to Yahweh. In these two rhetorical formations, the Second Temple appropriates the already established legitimacy of Solomon's temple, its cult, and the traditions attached to it. It thereby obscures any discontinuity between Solomon's temple and the one funded by the Persian crown. In this intentionality toward cultic legitimacy the rhetoric

---

not a destroyed item or person, but a possession devoted and sacrificed, given up for the use of God or his priests.

[43] Niditch, *War*, 60.

masks the social contradiction between historical and contemporary realities.

The subtext for the entire pericope of the divorce rhetoric is the Deuteronomic legislation against mixing with the inhabitants and their "abominations" mentioned throughout the Deuteronomistic literature. The Deuteronomic literature that inveighs against the inhabitants of Canaan is cast as Moses's exhortations to Israel in the Transjordan, while the divorce rhetoric appropriates the same Deuteronomic sermons. So at the outset the rhetoric casts the *golah* as ancient Israelites entering Canaan under the leadership of Joshua. Ezra 9:1 invokes the names of the traditional enemies of Israel against the "peoples of the lands." They are "as the Canaanites, Hittites, Perrizite, Jebusites, Ammonites, Moabites, Egyptians and Amorites." In Neh 13:1, the rhetoric almost directly quotes Deut 23:4[44] "...the book of Moses was read in the hearing of the people and in it was found written, that *neither a Moabite nor an Ammonite shall enter in the assembly of God.*" In the Deuteronomic rhetoric, however, the people are instructed to destroy the peoples of the lands.[45] In the divorce rhetoric of the Ezra-Nehemiah corpus they are admonished only against further intermarriage (Ezra 9, Nehemiah 10), or coerced to dissolve the marriages (Ezra 10, Nehemiah13). Not once does the rhetoric address the absence of most of these ethnic groups in the contemporaneous geopolitical context. Without comment or explanation, the rhetoric simply invokes them as a means of connecting this contemporary community with that of ancient Israel.

Second, Ezra 9–10 employs signs that connect the *golah* genealogically to ancient Israel. The rhetoric bridges any temporal or cultural gaps between the *golah* and ancient Israel by connecting the era of the kingdom of Judah to the era of Persian domination. Thus, Ezra 9:7 begins with the phrase, "From the days of our ancestors"; Nehemiah 10:39-40 refers to "a son of Aaron" and "sons of Levi"; and Nehemiah 13:26 alludes to the memory of King Solomon, claiming that he contended with the same sin. Just as the dominant language of the rhetoric held political meaning for the empire, the counter-knowledge of this alternative narrative deployed cultural symbols of the Second temple

---

[44] Deut 23:3 in English. [Emphasis added.]

[45] Deut 7:2.

community to communicate alternative values. For the Second Temple priesthood, it grounded their authority in divine authority and established Yahweh as sovereign even in the context of the imperial world. Its appropriation of the stories and personalities of Israelite history reinforced the identity of their community as heirs to ancient Israel and the people of Yahweh, not subjects of the empire.

Conclusion

By deploying cultural symbols within the rhetoric of Ezra 9-10, the Second Temple community communicates an alternative message to the Jerusalem community, one that resists the history and thus the identity of the "subjects" of the imperial story. This alternative identity is shaped by the community's life in Jerusalem more than their status as imperial subjects. The rhetoric supplants imperial authority with divine authority represented by the community's deity, Yahweh, rather than the crown. Second, the rhetoric differentiates the temple and its priesthood from those whose origin and authority are imperial. Instead, the rhetoric connects this temple and its community to the stories of the First Temple and Solomonic legitimation. It does so by deploying ritualistic performance. In moral and prescriptive forms, the ritual intends to transform their cosmological worldview from imperial sovereignty to Yahwistic sovereignty. Its kinesthetic performance encourages behaviors that orient the community toward this new identity.

Chapter 5

Subversive and Dominant Voices Elide: Economic Significations

Temples and Imperial Fiscal Administration

Two primary revenue streams comprised the imperial system's fiscal resources: tribute and land tenure. Temple complexes were central to both. Temple economies were also major economic producers in Babylon and in Egypt. Often temples controlled vast amounts of wealth, even dominating the economies in their locales. Larger temples, with more powerful and influential priesthoods, controlled immense areas of land known as latifundia, and counted hundreds of enslaved persons among their inventories.[1] Both the wealth that temple systems oversaw and the power that they mediated as unifying symbols incentivized the reigning monarchs to control them. Managing influential priesthoods and appropriating the surpluses from their wealthy temples were essential

---

[1] M. A. Dandamaev, "Neo-Babylonian Society and Economy," in *CAH:The Assyrian and Babylonian Empires and Other States of the Near East, from the Eighth to the Sixth Centuries B.C.* (ed. John Boardman, et al.; New York: Cambridge University Press, 1991), 270. Joseph Blenkinsopp argues, "Temples served as catalysts of economic exchange and promoters of social cohesion. The temple may also have been seen as a point of convergence for the symbolic structures of the region, an 'emblem of collective identity', thereby mitigating to some extent the inevitable resentment generated by subjection to a foreign power." Blenkinsopp, "Temple and Society," 26.

components of imperial fiscal administration. Successfully regulated, temples could be heavily taxed and become profitable sources of income for the crown.

As the empire expanded, collecting taxes meant raiding royal and temple treasuries upon conquest. There are reports that Cambyses routinely raided temple treasuries and seized temple wealth.[2] Although the practice diminished, it remained a threat for temples. As late as the reign of Artaxerxes III, Diodorus reports that on his campaign into Egypt, Artaxerxes III seized gold and other booty from Egyptian temples. Bagoas, who accompanied Artaxerxes III into Egypt, stole inscribed records and sold them back to the Egyptian priests for exorbitant amounts of money.[3] Unfortunately, imperial revenue-gathering raids required expensive military action and yielded only inconsistent revenue streams.

After the conquest of Egypt, westward expansion proved too costly and difficult as the Persian Empire competed with the Greek states for dominance in the region. As the empire turned from expansion as a primary source of revenue to intensifying their bureaucratic machine for collecting tribute and managing arable land, it developed a more efficient apparatus to administer the growing economy. Babylon and Memphis served as financial centers where imperial officials collected and stored taxes, some of which were used to provide lavish monetary or "in-kind" support for the satrap and his staff.[4] Each province had its own treasury

---

[2] Herodotus, *The History*. III.13, 89. See also M. A. Dandamaev, *Slavery in Babylonia from Nabopolassar to Alexander the Great (626-331 B.C.)* (Northern Illinois University Press, 1984), 107-08. See also Christopher Tuplin, "Darius' Suez Canal and Persian Imperialism," *Achaemenid History* 6 (1991): 237-83.

[3] See Diodorus, *Library of History*, XVI.51.2 (Oldfather, LCL).

[4] Some satraps acquired huge tracts of property in their jurisdictions where they erected lavish residences. Arsames, who held office during the reign of Artaxerxes II Mnemnon, held properties throughout Egypt. An Elephantine letter mentions his properties in Lower Egypt and reports that they were managed by a *peqid*, who commanded a company of soldiers to protect the satrapal holdings. Satraps often would appropriate agricultural surpluses to be used by their staff or by the garrisons that protected their residences. Porten and Yardeni, *Textbook of Aramaic Documents from Ancient Egypt*, A:6.7, A:6.8 and A:6.10.

with its treasurers, bookkeepers, and treasury scribes. The scribes were connected to "the king's house," which was a government warehouse for storing goods paid in kind as tribute. On occasion, goods were drawn from this king's house to supplement mercenary wages and rations.[5] Officials known as *pakhuta* carried out such routine functions distributing monetary and "in-kind" revenues from the satrapal treasuries[6] under the supervision of a *gan-za-ba-ru*, a position closely approximating that of a satrapal or provincial treasurer.[7]

Although the satrap was supreme, these other imperial officials checked his administrative decisions, as a 421 B.C.E. series of Aramaic papyri documenting the meticulous nature of the administration of satrapal funds attests. The papyri report, for example, that Arsames, the satrap of Egypt, received notice that one of the boats in Persian service on the Nile needed repair. He ordered a certain Wahprimahi, also in government employ, to make repairs to it. In turn, Wahprimahi sent the order to treasury officials who inspected the boat to ensure that the repairs were actually necessary. Finding the boat indeed in need of repair, the treasury officials kept a careful accounting of exactly the quantity and type of supplies used for the work.[8]

With the same attention to detail, the satrap and lesser officials intervened in the financial affairs of local cults. From Babylon and Memphis, Persian satraps, governors, and other imperial officials sent orders for goods and services produced by temples to be paid to the crown. Imperial officials closely monitored the agricultural production of

---

[5] E. Bresciani, "The Persian Occupation of Egypt," in *The Cambridge History of Iran: Volume 2 The Median and Achaemenian Periods* (ed. Ilya Gerschevitch; New York: Cambridge University Press, 1985), 515 n 3 and 4.

[6] Porten, *The Elephantine Papyri*, B11. The papyrus, which I discuss below, details the bureaucratic levels involved in a simple boat repair.

[7] Cameron, *Persepolis Treasure Tablets*, 214. Stolper, *Entrepreneurs and Empire: The Murasu Archive, the Murasu Firm, and Persian Rule in Babylonia*, 139. See also Tavernier 4.4.7.49.

[8] Porten, *The Elephantine Papyri*, B11. The papyrus reports the occasion of a boat leased in government service in need of repair. At least four levels of bureaucracy, satrapal, local treasury, storehouse authorities, and imperial craftsmen participate in certifying the need and repairing the boat.

temples and protected imperial interests by ensuring that the portions of temple surpluses requested in taxes were sent to royal residences throughout the empire.[9] In Babylonia, these orders generally included the phrase, "If not, he will incur the punishment of Gu-ba-ru-'."[10] Gu-ba-ru-' was the satrap of Ebr-Nahara and Babylonia, and closely regulated temple financial affairs. He received notification from temples about the number of enslaved persons who had died or had escaped and enforced the punishment of persons who had stolen temple property. On one occasion, he punished shepherds who were responsible for the temple's failure to provide its requirement of sheep and cattle to the empire. In Egypt, a Demotic papyrus reports a decree by Cambyses that ordered the diminution of the funding of all except three local temples.[11] Under Darius I, the imperial bureaucratic structure became more orderly with regularized tax collection. A Demotic document from 486 B.C.E. reports that officials from the sanctuary at Elephantine were compelled to make payments into the account of Parnu, the Persian official.[12] Herodotus reports that Darius required all provinces to pay the monetary portion of their taxes in silver and determined the amount of the levy based upon the area of land that each province cultivated.[13] Babylonia contributed 1,000 talents of silver annually to the Persian treasury.[14] Egypt was assessed an annual tribute of 700 talents, 120,000 bushels of grain, and all of the profits realized from the fisheries at Lake Moeris; had to maintain the Persian and foreign soldiers stationed at the White Fort in Memphis; and, as Athenaeus reports, was required to supply the emperor

---

[9] Dandamaev, *Iranians in Achaemenid Babylonia*, 19-20.

[10] For example, see the Dandamaev and Lukonin translation of GCCI, II 120. Uruk VIII/12/2, Cambyses (6 November 528). Dandamaev et al., *The Culture and Social Institutions of Ancient Iran*, 362-63.

[11] Spiegelberg, *Die sogenannte demotische Chronik des Pap. 215 der Bibliothèque Nationale du Paris*.

[12] Martin, "The Demotic Texts," C4.

[13] Herodotus, *The History*, III.89. While Herodotus's figures are clearly not accurate, they do account for a regularized system of revenue in the imperial system.

[14] Herodotus, *The History*, III.92.

with table salt and Nile water.[15] These latter two tributes were symbols of fealty to the Persian pharaoh.

Agrarian Economy and the Achaemenid Land Tenure

For the empire, leveraging land tenure was as important as managing tributes. In both Babylonia and Egypt, Achaemenid kings took possession of vast tracts of the richest arable land for official purposes, such as building palatial satrapal and provincial residences. These buildings served as royal archives, storehouses for petitions to the satrap, satrapal resolutions, and centers for the regional bureaucracy.[16] Beyond official use, however, the Persians rented out this land in exchange for service or payment. In Babylon, the crown leased the richest arable land to aristocrats and to banking firms like the Murashu, which, in turn, leased the land for profit and compensated the empire with an annual base rent and a portion of the produce. Land with easy access to water fetched higher rents than parcels more remotely located.[17] Land tenure in the form of military fiefs compensated soldiers for military service. [18]

---

[15] Herodotus, *The History*, III.91. See also Athenaeus II.67b.

[16] Kuhrt, *The Ancient Near East c. 3000-330 BC*, 691-92.

[17] Stolper, *Entrepreneurs and Empire*, 125-34. Stolper argues that the difference in rental price for land varied greatly depending upon that parcel's access to water.

[18] In Babylonia, the Persians granted military fiefs in three kinds: bow fiefs, chariot fiefs, and cavalry fiefs. Stolper, *Entrepreneurs and Empire* 25. Briant adds "hand estate" (*'bit ritti*). Briant, 75.These fiefs were grounded in the imperial right to all conquered land. They extended from the lines of Cyrus and Cambyses and could be withdrawn at will. The crown granted these fiefs to soldiers in exchange for service as needed in the imperial army. Soldiers enjoyed land tenure tax-free during their service. However, during times when no military service was required, the grantees had to pay a tax to the crown. Stolper, *Entrepreneurs and Empire*, 24-27. In Egypt, the Persians encountered an Egyptian military class that already had vast land holdings. Herodotus reports that its members owned two-thirds of the delta region, the most fertile land in the region. Herodotus, followed by others, thinks they numbered around 410,000. Herodotus, *The History,* II.165–8 (Greene). Since supporting large numbers of troops with land tenure and other means of compensation placed a huge strain on the economy, military administration was as much an economic

Temples received land grants as well. Since Egyptian temples held tenure to huge tracts of land, taxes levied upon those lands became sources of income.[19] In Babylon, the crown had already instituted an effective system of monetizing temple land grants before the Persians arrived. Within the first two years of his reign, Nabonidus changed Babylonian policy toward temple administration and seized control of temple wealth. He created two offices for administering temple wealth[20] in the service of the monarch. In 555, Nabonidus visited southern Babylonia and enacted an extensive reorganization of the Eanna there,[21] with reforms that granted temple personnel land tenure in return for a portion of the produce. Nabonidus' son, Belshazzar, created the *fermier générale, a* system that placed acres of farmland under the authority of either a single person or a small group, with the understanding that the "chief farmer" would reserve for the crown an allotted quantity of dates

---

matter as it was a matter of imperial security. In total, the standing army probably consisted of 12,000 men. Bezalel Porten, *Archives from Elephantine: The Life of an Ancient Jewish Military Colony* (Berkeley: University of California Press, 1968), 62-72. The more pressing concern for the empire, however, was managing an army comprising warriors of varied ethnicities and ensuring that they remained loyal to Persia.

[19] Based on the instances of donation stelas, Dimitri Meeks shows that royal gifts to temples in Egypt disappeared after the twenty-sixth dynasty and did not resume until the Hellenistic period. See Dimitri Meeks, "Les donations aux temples dans l'Égypte du Ier millénaire avant J.-C.," in *State and Temple Economy in the Ancient Near East* (ed. E. Lipinski; Louvain: Departement Orientalistiek, 1979).

[20] On one occasion, Nabonidus made a gift to several temples simultaneously of 2,850 males held in slavery. He also gave gifts to the temple in Ur consisting of enslaved persons, land, and livestock (Dandamaev, "Neo-Babylonian Society and Economy," 269).

[21] In a text dated to April 27, 555 B.C.E. (*YOS* VI:11), Nabonidus granted Kalba and Sum-ukin the right to cultivate land belonging to the Eanna of Uruk. In return they were to designate a portion of their harvest for the temple complex. Cited from Beaulieu, *The Reign of Nabonidus: King of Babylon 556-539 B.C.*, 117-21.

and grains.[22] At every stage, royal commissioners checked the work of the chief farmer to ensure that the interests of the royal family, and later those of the empire, were protected. When the Persians arrived in Babylon, they simply exchanged officials loyal to the former Neo-Babylonian regime for those of Persian ethnicity, and appropriated temple surpluses for imperial use.

Following their Babylonian predecessors, Persian kings granted land tenure and enslaved persons to temples as well. Using these human and natural resources, temples, in return, produced huge agricultural surpluses, increasing the value of the land to the crown and, of course, the taxable wealth in their inventories. Since the Persians extracted significant revenues from Babylonian temples, they also assisted temples in amassing wealth, even going so far as to punish thieves who stole from them. At the same time, they increased fiscal pressure on temples by not tithing to them, as did their Babylonian predecessors.[23] Instead, the Persians required temples to pay taxes in silver or in kind to the Achaemenid kings. These tributes comprised all manner of produce, including sheep, goats, cattle, barley, sesame, dates, wine, beer, spices, oil, butter, milk, wool, provisions for state officials, and laborers for the royal estates. Moreover, the Persians demanded that temples provide enslaved persons—farmers, herdsman, gardeners, and carpenters—for service on royal estates.[24] Often the taxes levied against temple surpluses placed severe hardship on temple economies. For example, during the second regnal year of Cambyses, the Eanna at Uruk was required to deliver provisions to the royal estate at Abanu. In order to fulfill the request, the temple was forced to go into debt for large amounts of silver.[25]

---

[22] Similar to the grant made by his father a decade earlier, Belshazzar grants Ibni-Istar the privilege of cultivating a tract of land belonging to the Eanna. Again, the grant obligated the grantee to return a portion of the produce to the crown. See Beaulieu, *The Reign*, 193-4.

[23] Dandamaev, *Iranians in Achaemenid Babylonia*, 19-20.

[24] Dandamaev, "Achaemenid Babylonia," 309-10.

[25] Briant, *From Cyrus to Alexander*, 73.

Temple Administration in Jerusalem

Now we have sufficient background information to ask: would the empire go to great expense to fund the construction of a temple in Jerusalem unless its economic function was to be similarly revenue-producing to that of other temples throughout the empire? Would the Jerusalem temple and its priesthood be exempted from fiscal pressures imposed upon other temples? How could its priesthood, with few material resources, respond to policies of imperial temple administration?

There is no evidence that the Jerusalem temple was granted special dispensation by the imperial system.[26] It would have been required to meet taxation targets set for it just as they were set for any other Achaemenid temple. That burden must have increased significantly when later kings desperately needed revenue to fund a far-flung and protracted war against the Greeks. Yehud was a small, poor province. Its economic resources were few. Operating under a foreign tributary economy much of what little surplus it produced would have been directed to fund the imperial system. This factor impacted the temple in Jerusalem more significantly than it impacted larger temples with more extensive agricultural and human resources, like those of the Eanna in Babylonia and at Saïs in Egypt. While those temples also struggled under burdensome Persian policies of economic depletion, the temple in Jerusalem struggled to a far greater extent.

Studies have speculated about the sources of revenue for Yehud's temple. Since the temple was the center of a small province, several studies have argued that it was more directly connected to the imperial fiscal administrative apparatus than other temples. For example, Joachim Schaper argues that at least two systems of taxation were operative in the Jerusalem temple. One set of funds—the *midda, belo,* and *halak*, identified by Aramaic names—comprised the "king's chest" and went directly to the satrap, while the other—the *teruma*, identified

---

[26] Lester L. Grabbe, "The Law of Moses and the Ezra Tradition: More Virtual Than Real?," in *Persia and Tora: The Theory of Imperial Authorization of the Pentateuch* (ed. James L. Watts; *SBLSymS* 17; Atlanta: Society of Biblical Literature, 2001), 110. See more recently, Lester L. Grabbe, "The "Persian Documents" in the Book of Ezra: Are They Authentic?," in *Judah and Judeans in the Persian Period* (ed. Oded Lipschits and Manfred Oeming; Winona Lake, In.: Eisenbrauns, 2006).

with Hebrew nomenclature—was meant for the temple.[27] The distinction makes clear that a substantial portion of the revenue collected was deposited into imperial treasuries.

Moreover, the Jerusalem temple system was subject to shifts in the economic policies of the crown. The two decades of Xerxes's reign brought dramatic changes in relation to imperial authorities. Xerxes's policies of economic depletion stood in contradistinction to Darius's fiscally generous policy of funding some local temples. The death of Darius I left a huge power vacuum, and revolts sprang up throughout the Achaemenid Empire. Xerxes responded quickly and decisively to restore order by violently putting down revolts and destroying temples.[28] As part of his economic policy, he increased taxation, shifting the bulk of the tax burden to non-Persians. Additionally, he removed non-Persians from administrative positions. By withholding funds from local cults, Xerxes solidified Persian control and effected the ascendancy of Persian ethnicity. His successor, Artaxerxes I, inherited an empire in severe economic decline, strained by Xerxes's policies of depletion. If an emissary such as Ezra arrived in Yehud, along with imperial funding, in the seventh year of Artaxerxes I's reign, 458 B.C.E.,[29] that may have indicated a change in imperial economic policy. For the empire, the investment in the Jerusalem temple complex whether in the form of land,

---

[27] Joachim Schaper, "The Jerusalem Temple as an Instrument of the Achaemenid Fiscal Administration," *VT* 45/4 (1995): 529-39.

[28] His destruction of local cults decreased the volatile nationalistic sentiments in these locales. Kuhrt and Sherwin-White, "Xerxes' Destruction of Babylonian Temples," 70. See also Olmstead, *A History of the Persian Empire*, 210-46.

[29] The dating of Ezra's arrival in Yehud has been a source of much debate by scholars. For a later dating, see Miller and Hayes, *A History of Ancient Israel and Judah*, 468. See also Ahlström, *The History of Ancient Palestine*, 874ff. For an overview of the debate see pp. 88-92. See also Berquist, *Judaism in Persia's Shadow*, 110. This study assumes the traditional dating of the construction of the temple in 515 under the reign of Darius I. But see the recent persuasive argument of Diana Edelman. She dates the Temple to the twentieth year of Artaxerxes I in *The Origins of the 'Second' Temple: Persian Imperial Policy and the Rebuilding of Jerusalem* (London: Equnox, 2005). If her argument is correct, then the pressures on the Second Temple would have been intensified by escalating conflicts with the Greeks, in particular Artaxerxes's practice of funding the enemies of the Greeks.

funds for building materials, or laborers was no different than funding that had been directed toward larger temple complexes in Babylonia or Egypt. Attention from imperial authorities always meant an increased economic strain on local communities. This attention signaled neither a period of economic abundance nor imperial generosity but rather it sought to increase imperial revenue. Land was to be cultivated to provide in-kind tribute such as supplies for the imperial military and provincial authorities. Likewise, buildings were erected primarily to accommodate official administrative needs and only secondarily for local use. Laborers were conscripted to expedite imperial tasks. Any resources that flowed to the temple were to raise its capacity for production and thus increase its imperial tax levy. So while the imperial system experienced an uptick in revenue due to its local investment, it was at the expense of the Second Temple community.

Jerusalem's Temple:
Constructing Ideologies of Ethnicity and Gender

For the Second Temple priesthood, surplus flowing to imperial treasuries therefore meant there was less to support the Temple's activities. Temple rituals would diminish, as would the priesthood's capacity to compete with any locally functioning cults. While the Second Temple priesthood could not influence the policies of the empire, it could legislate local policies and appropriate symbolic resources, such as its ability to effect normative constructs of ethnic identity and gender roles, to control as much as possible the flow of material resources within the community.

Both ethnicity and gender carried economic consequences for the Jerusalem community depending on how the Second Temple priesthood erected boundaries for in-group and out-group designations and constructed roles for marriage and family life. Much has been written about the question of ethnicity in the early Second Temple period; it need not be rehearsed here.[30] Ethnic purity as an ideology regulated access to

---

[30] Randall C. Bailey has written the seminal critical study for ethnicity and ideology. See Randall C. Bailey, "They're Nothing but Incestuous Bastards: The Polemical Use of Sex and Sexuality in Hebrew Canon Narratives," in *Reading from this Place: Social Location and Biblical Interpretation in the United States*, (ed. Fernando F. Segovia and Mary Ann Tolbert; Minneapolis: Fortress Press, 1995), 121-38; Smith-Christopher, "Between Ezra and Isaiah: Exclusion, Trans-formation, and Inclusion of the 'Foreigner' in Post-Exilic Biblical Theology;"

the political and social power. The cult itself was jealously guarded to prevent the incursion of outside membership. For the Second Temple community, ethnic identity comprised two structures, one ideological and one genealogical. First, in mimetic appropriation of the conquest stories under Joshua's leadership, the golah were those who returned to an "empty" land promised to them.[31] Those outside of the *golah* community were typified as the enemies of this new Israel. These new enemies, the *'am ha'arets*, were taken up as analogues to Israel's traditional enemies (Deut 7:1-6; Ezra 9:1-2). Second, ethnic purity meant belonging to a *bet 'abot*, the official registry of kinship structures in Ez 2 and Neh 7. The registries preserved power for cultic elites and other members of the Jerusalem aristocracy. Their fictive kinship rosters organized the community with a clearly delineated social structure and fiercely maintained boundaries of inclusion and exclusion between the *bene haggolah* and *'am ha'arets*.

Gender as well as ethnicity carried economic consequences. Post-exilic society's increased stratification based on gender eroded the former, and perhaps more egalitarian social structures, of course, at the expense of women.[32] With the ascendency of the Second Temple

---

Eskenazi and Judd, "Marriage to a Stranger in Ezra 9-10;" Charles B. Copher, "The Black Presence in the Old Testament," in *Stony the Road We Trod: African American Biblical Interpretation* (ed. Cain Hope Felder; Minneapolis: Fortress Press, 1991); Rodney S. Sadler Jr., *Can a Cushite Change His Skin? An Examination of Race, Ethnicity, and Othering in the Hebrew Bible*, JSOTSup 425 (New York/London: T&T Clark, 2005); Jacob L. Wright, "Surviving in an Imperial Context: Foreign Military Service and Judean Identity," in *Judah and Judeans in the Achaemenid Period* (ed. Oded Lipschits, Gary N. Knoppers, and Manfred Oeming; Winona Lake, In.: Eisenbrauns, 2011); Rainer Albertz, "The Controversy about Judean versus Israelite Identity," in *Judah and Judeans in the Achaemenid Period* (ed. Oded Lipschits, Gary N. Knoppers, and Manfred Oeming; Winona Lake, In.: Eisenbrauns, 2011).

[31]Ahlström, *The History of Ancient Palestine*, 823. See also Carroll, "The Myth of the Empty Land."

[32] Claudia Camp, Carole Fontaine, and Gale A. Yee have done the seminal work in this area in their fine studies. Claudia V. Camp's study of the female sage analyzes the roles of women in monarchic Israel and the Persian and Hellenistic Periods. See her "The Female Sage in Ancient Israel and in the Biblical Wisdom Literature," in *The Sage in Israel and the Ancient Near East* (ed. John G. Gammie and Leo G. Perdue; Winona Lake: Eisenbrauns, 1990), 185–203.

community came the reinscription of values and mores, subjecting women to their *bet 'abot*. Women's access to public authority was severely limited in comparison to earlier eras. Further, this increased stratification and role definition extended especially into the realm of sexuality, and consigned a woman's sexuality to the pleasure of her husband.[33] Women outside the Second Temple community would not have been governed by these mores. It would be virtually impossible to compel so-called "foreign" women (those who were not devotees of the Second Temple) to adhere to "Israelite" law.[34] Without a husband and without ties to a *bet 'abot*, a "foreign" woman might be freer (if she were not beholden to another cultural system) than a woman of the *golah* to deploy her sexuality for her own pleasure in the fashion she chose. The "foreign" woman under Persian rule was then a liminal figure in

---

Carole R. Fontaine, "The Social Roles of Women in the World of Wisdom," in *A Feminist Companion to Wisdom Literature* (ed. Athalya Brenner; Sheffield: Sheffield Academic Press, 1995), 35-36. See also the broad study by Gale A. Yee, *Poor Banished Children of Eve* (Minneapolis: Fortress, 2003). See also Carol Meyers, *Discovering Eve: Ancient Israelite Women in Context* (New York: Oxford University Press, 1988). Meyers argues for more egalitarian societal arrangements in the Levant before the rise of the public sphere and the eclipse of the domestic sphere.

[33] Concerning Hebrew wives, Phyllis Bird argues, "She defers to him [her husband] in speech and action, obeys his wish as his command, and puts his welfare first. She employs her sexual gifts for his pleasure alone...." Phyllis Bird, *Missing Persons and Mistaken Idenitites: Women and Gender in Ancient Israel* (Minneapolis: Fortress, 1997), 38.

[34] In Ezra-Nehemiah, the laws' subjects are members of the community. In Ezra 9:1, Ezra is concerned that "the people of Israel, the priests and the Levites" have not separated themselves from the people of the lands. In 10:9 Ezra's concern is that "all the people of Judah and Benjamin" have broken the law of Moses. In Nehemiah, Ezra reads the law to the "people of Israel" in 7:73. In Nehemiah 13:23, Nehemiah's reforms are directed toward the "Jews." For an in-depth analysis of the effects of biblical laws on women in the ancient world, see the well-done study by Cheryl B. Anderson, *Women, Ideology and Violence: Critical Theory and the Construction of Gender in the Book of the Covenant and the Deuteronomic Law* (New York: Continuum, 2004).

Jerusalem; she possessed more autonomy than her *golah* counterpart but was still subject, nonetheless, to the imperial authority.[35]

Consequently, in a society that maintained order and genealogically circumscribed in-group/out-group designations, these liminal women and the men who blurred genealogical structures by marrying them or by sexual association with them, were dangerous to the Second Temple elite. By associating with "foreign" women, these men widened the circle of those who had access to power and influence over the affairs of the *golah* community.[36]

In concert with imperial political interests, postexilic Jerusalem maintained strict control over ethnicity, gender, and sexuality. Succinctly put, men whose *bet 'abot* was listed and landed had access to power. Women, on the whole, were subordinate in the *bet 'abot*, and a woman's sexuality was to be controlled by her husband. A "foreign" woman on the other hand, one whom the *golah* probably associated with the *'am ha 'arets*, that is one whose sexuality, culture, and access to wealth[37] were

---

[35] For a study of the freedoms that women in Egypt and Mesopotamia possessed particularly as it related to owning property, see the insightful article by Annalisa Azzoni, "Women and Property in Persian Egypt and Mesopotamia" (paper presented at the Colloquium on Women and Property in Ancient Near Eastern and Mediterranean Societies, The Center for Hellenic Studies-Harvard University, 2002).

[36] See Harold Washington, who makes a similar case concerning Proverbs 1–9. Harold Washington, "The Strange Woman (*issah zara/nokriyah*) of Proverbs 1-9," in *A Feminist Companion to Wisdom Literature* (ed. Athalya Brenner; FCB 9; Sheffield: Sheffield Academic Press, 1995).

[37] Concerning the foreign women in Proverbs 7, for instance, Van der Toorn has argued that these women outside the Israelite cult, who had neither a father nor a husband willing to meet their obligations for them, were often forced to resort to prostitution in order to pay their vows. However, this does not seem to be the case for the *isshah zara* of Proverbs 7. K. van der Toorn, "Female Prostitution and the Payment of Vows in Ancient Israel," *JBL* 108 (1989): 193-205. Bailey has argued that possession of the spices indicates wealth in the ancient world. See also Randall C. Bailey, "Beyond Identification: The Use of Africans in Old Testatment Poetry and Narratives," in *Stony the Road We Trod: African American Biblical Interpretation* (ed. Cain Hope Felder; Minneapolis: Fortress Press, 1991). See also Claudia V. Camp, "The Female Sage in Ancient Israel and in the Biblical Wisdom Literature," in *The Sage in Israel and the Ancient*

not directed by the mores of the Second Temple, was a serious threat to the nascent aristocracy struggling to create ethnic cohesion and to maintain its legitimacy in the eyes of the empire.

To maintain power under imperial dominion, the *golah* community constructed their existence over against groups. The phenomena that gave rise to the construction of these significations were a complex set of historical events both internal and external to the province. They included the institution of a foreign tributary economy that fueled imperial expansion, the influx of new populations and the increased competition for resources, the onset of new social stratification, and burdensome imperial system. In the economic signification of the divorce rhetoric, the Second Temple priesthood responds to complex turn of events in Jerusalem. At an economic level, the divorce rhetoric becomes a central component of the Second Temple's effort to enlist its community's support against imperial repression.

Analyzing the Rhetoric:
   Converging Imperial and Community Interests
   The economic significance of the divorce rhetoric has to do with the realities of a temple struggling under the burden of imperial taxation. In this context, the most significant function of intermarriage is its ability to transfer property, and thus wealth and status, from one group to another. Admonitions against intermarriage served to maintain land tenure within the group. More specifically, practicing exogamy had the potential to alienate land from the families of the *golah*. The transfer of land to families who were not a part of the temple community, or to those who were not adherents of the religion of Yahweh, would shift the balance of wealth and power between social groups and would leave the *golah* further impoverished.

The divorce rhetoric of Nehemiah 10 and 13 reflects struggles for control of material resources in the economic realm of Yehud. Neh 10 narrates concerns that are dramatized by Nehemiah in Neh 13: 4-31: the rejection of exogamy and the centrality of the house of God. In the economic signification, dominant and subversive languages work in tandem to fortify the financial resources of the Second Temple temple. The dominant language of Nehemiah informs the Persians that this

---

Near East (ed. John G. Gammie and Leo G. Perdue; Winona Lake, Ind.: Eisenbrauns, 1990).

temple, like its counterparts throughout the imperial system is dutifully raising funds to meet its tax levy. Its subversive language calls the Second Temple community to support the "house of God" as a symbol of cultural and religious survival; it is a counter-narrative of resistance.

Author's Translation of Nehemiah 10 and 13
Nehemiah 10

1. And because of all of this we make a permanent agreement in writing and upon the seal are [the names of] our officials, our Levites, and our priests.

2. And upon the seal are Nehemiah, the governor, son of Haclaiah, and Zedekiah,

3. Seraiah, Azariah, Jeremiah,

4. Pashhur, Amariah, Malchijah,

5. Hattush, Shebaniah, Malluch,

6. Harim, Meremoth, Obadiah,

7. Daniel, Ginnithon, Baruch,

8. Meshullam, Abiah, Mijamin,

9. Maaziah, Bilgai, and Shemaiah; these are the priests.

10. And the Levites: Jeshua, son of Azaniah, Binui of the descendants of Henadad, Kadmiel;

11. And their brothers: Shebanaiah, Hodiah, Kelita, Pelaiah Hanan,

12. Mica, Rahob, Hashbiah,

13. Zaccur, Sherebiah, Shebaniah,

14. Hodiah, Bani, and Beninu.

15. The leaders of the people: Paroah, Pahath-moab, Elam, Zattu, Bani,

16. Buni,[38] Azggad, Benai,

17. Adonijah, Bigvai, Adin

18. Ater, Hezekaiah, Azzur,

19. Hodiah, Hashum, Bezai,

20. Hariph, Anathoth, Nebai,

21. Magpiash, Meshullam, Hezir,

22. Meshezabel, Zadok, Jaddua,

---

[38] LXX reads Bani.

23. Pelatiah, Hanan, and Anaiah,

24. Hoshea, Hananiah, Hasshub,

25. Hallohesh, Pilha, Shobek,

26. Rehum, Hashabnah, Maaseiah,

27. Ahiah, Hanan, Anan,

28. Malluch, Harim, and Baanah.

29. And the rest of the people, the priest the Levites, the gatekeepers, the singers, the persons enslaved for the temple, and all who separated themselves from the peoples of the lands to the law of God, with their wives, their sons, and their daughters, and all who have knowledge and understanding.

30. Join[39] with their brothers, their dignitaries (nobles) and entering into an oath and a curse to do according to the law of God, which was given by the hand of Moses, servant of God, to keep and to do all the commandments of the Lord, our Lord and his ordinances and statutes.

31. We will not give our daughters to the people of the land nor take for our sons their daughters.

32. And when the people of the land bring in wares or grain on the Sabbath to sell, we will not take it from them on a sabbath day or a holy day. And we will let the fields lie fallow on the seventh year and forgo the exaction of any debt.

33. And we will place upon ourselves the duty to charge ourselves one-third of a shekel per year to serve the house of our God.

34. For the rows of bread and for the continual grain offerings, for the burnt offerings, the sabbaths, the new moons, the festivals,[40] and the sacred donations, the sin offerings to make expiation for Israel, and for all the works of the house of our God.

35. And we have cast lots among the priests, the Levites, and the people, for the wood offering to bring it to the house of the Lord, our God, by fathers' houses at appointed times year by year to burn upon the altar of the Lord, our God, as it is written in the law.

36. And to bring the first fruits of our soil and the first fruits of all the fruit of every tree, year by year, to the house of the Lord.

---

[39] MT literally, "were strong."

[40] Literally, "appointed times."

37. And to bring to the house of our God, to the priests who minister in the house of our God. The firstborn of our sons and our beasts, as it is written in the law, and the first of our cattle and sheep;

38. And the first of our grain and our contributions, and the fruit of every tree, the new wine and the oil we will bring to the priest to the treasuries of the house of our God; and to bring to the Levites the tithes from our soil; for the Levites are the ones who are given the tithes in all our cities of our labor.

39. And the priest, a son of Aaron, will be with the Levites when the Levites receive the tithe; and the Levites shall bring up a tithe of the tithe to the house of our God, to the chambers of the treasury.

40. For the people of Israel, and the sons of Levi, will bring the contribution of grain, wine, and oil, to the chambers where the holy vessels are and where the priests who minister, and the gatekeepers, and the singers are. We will not forsake the house of our God.

Nehemiah 13

1. On that day, the book of Moses[41] was read in hearing of the people, and in it was found written that neither a Moabite nor an Ammonite shall enter the assembly of God for ever,

2. because they did not meet the children of Israel with bread and water, but hired Balaam to curse them; but our God turned the curse into a blessing.

3. And so it was, as they heard the law, they separated all the foreigners from Israel.

4. But before this, Eliashib, the priest who was placed over the chambers of the house of our God, was related to Tobiah.

5. And he made for him a large, room and there before they had placed the grain offering, the frankincense, the vessels, the tithes of grain, the wine, and the oil, which were [given by] commandment to the Levites, the singers, the gatekeepers, and the contributions [to the] priests.

---

[41] A few Hebrew manuscripts read "book of the law of Moses." However, an emendation is unnecessary since "book of Moses" has the same connotation.

6. For all of this, I was not in Jerusalem, for in the thirty-second year of Artaxerxes, king of Babylon, I went to the king. And the end of some days, I asked [leave of] the king.

7. And I came to Jerusalem, and I discerned the evil that Eliashib had done for Tobiah, making for him a room in the courts[42] of the house of God.

8. And this was very displeasing to me, and I cast out all of the articles of Tobiah out of the room.

9. Then I gave the order, and they returned the vessels of the house of God with the grain offering and the frankincense.

10. And I discovered that the portions of the Levites had not been given[43] to them so that the Levites and the singers, who had rendered service, had fled to their fields.

11. So I contended with the prefects and said, "Why is the house of God forsaken?" And I gathered them, and I stood them on their standing-places.

12. And all of Judah brought the tithe of grain, wine, and oil to the treasuries.

13. And I appointed as treasurers[44] over the treasuries Shelemiah, the priest, and the scribes Zadok and Pediah from the Levites, and as their assistant, Hanan, son of Zaccur, son of Mattaniah, for they were reckoned trustworthy. Upon them was the task of distributing to their brothers.

14. Remember me, O my God, on account of this and do not wipe out my good deeds; which I have done in the house of my God and for its service.

15. In those days I saw them in Judah treading wine-presses and bringing heaps of produce and loading them upon donkeys; and also

---

[42] Some Hebrew manuscripts, the LXX and Syriac, read the singular. This may be an attempt to exaggerate the size of the temple in response to the disappointment that it did not compare with the size of Solomon's temple.

[43] With *Qere.*

[44] Following Torrey, who argues that the word has financial connotations. See C. C. Torrey, "The Evolution of a Financier in the Ancient Near East," *JNES* 2 (1943): 295-301; and C. C. Torrey, "The Foundry of the Second Temple at Jerusalem," *JBL* 55 (1936): 247-60.

wine, grapes, figs, and all loads and bringing them to Jerusalem on the Sabbath day. And I warned[45] them[46] in that day against selling food.

16. Tyrians who lived in the city brought fish and all merchandise and sold on the Sabbath to the children of Judah.

17. And I contended with the nobles of Judah, and I said to them, "What is this evil that you have done, profaning the Sabbath day?"

18. Did not your ancestors do thusly, and did not our God bring distress upon us and upon this city? You add more wrath upon Israel by profaning the Sabbath.

19. And so it was as it became dark[47] at the gates of Jerusalem before the Sabbath, I ordered the doors shut and I ordered that they should not be opened until after the Sabbath. And I set some of my young boys (servants) upon the gates so that[48]no load would enter on the Sabbath day.

20. And the traders and merchants of all kinds of merchandise spent the night outside Jerusalem once or twice.

21. And I admonished them, and I said to them, "Why would you spend the night in front of the wall? If you repeat this, I will beat you with my hands (lit. send my hand against you)." From that time on, they did not come on the Sabbath.

22. And I commanded the Levites that they should purify themselves and come and guard the gates to consecrate the Sabbath day as holy. Remember me in this also my God and look with compassion upon me according to your great kindness.

23. In those days, I saw Jews (Judahites) who had married women of Ashdod, Ammon, and Moab,

---

[45] Literally, "bore witness against."

[46] The MT lacks an object for the verb, so the Syriac is preferable here.

[47] Cf. Blenkinsopp who argues that this is poorly attested and reads with Godfrey Rolls Driver, "Hebrew Homonyms," *VTSup* 16 (1967): 62-63. NEB "when quiet had returned to the gates of Jerusalem." Meyers translates as "emptied." Jacob Meyers, *Ezra Nehemiah* (ed. William Foxwell Albright and David Noel Freedman; New York: Doubleday, 1965).

[48] Adding with several Hebrew manuscripts.

24. and half of their children did not regard[49] the language of Judah, but spoke the language of Ashdod.

25. And I contended with them, and I cursed them, and I struck some of the men and pulled out their hair. Then I made them take an oath in the name of God, "You shall not give your daughters to their sons, and you shall not take their daughters for your sons or for yourselves.

26. Did not King Solomon of Israel sin, and there was no king great like him among the nations? And, was he loved by his God, and God set him king over all Israel and even so the foreign women caused him to sin?

27. Shall we listen to you and do all this great evil, acting unfaithfully against our God by marrying foreign women?

28. And one of the sons of Jehoiada, son of the high priest Eliashib, was the son-in-law of the Horonite, Sanballat. I made him flee from my presence.

29. Remember them, my God, on account of this—they have defiled the priesthood, the covenant of the priesthood and the Levites.

30. Thus I cleansed them from all that was foreign and I established the functions of the priest and the Levites; each one in his work

31. and for the wood offering at the appointed time for the first fruits. Remember me, my God, for good.

Nehemiah 10 is cast as a response to the question raised in Nehemiah 9. In Nehemiah 9, the priesthood framed the problem as *Heilsgeschichte*: the creation (9:6), the promise of Abraham (9:7-8), the Exodus, the call of Moses, the giving of the law at Sinai (9:9-15), the wilderness wandering (9:19-21), and the conquest of the land. Interspersed among the recollection of Yahweh's saving acts is a lament for the "wickedness" of their ancestors and an affirmation of Yahweh's

---

[49] While the NRSV translates the phrase as "could not speak," in Deut 21:17, Isa 63:16, and 61:9 the sense of the Hifil is "to be willing to recognize." In Gen 31:32, 37:32, 38:25; Job 34:25 and Ruth 2:10, 19 the sense of the Hifil "is "to pay attention to" or "regard." Here, I leave these two connotations in tension, to argue that the reason the offspring disregarded the language of the Judahites is because they were captivated by the wealth of the maternal families.

faithfulness despite the disobedience of Israel. The chapter culminates (vv. 35-37) with a critique of the current social reality in light of the unfaithfulness of the ancestors:

> Here we are slaves to this day—slaves in the land that you gave to our ancestors, to enjoy its fruit and its good gifts. Its rich yield goes to the kings whom you have set over us because of our sins; they have power also over our bodies, and over our livestock at their pleasure, and we are in great distress.

This final statement of chapter 9[50] makes the problem, the great distress, clear; it is Persian control over *golah* wealth—even the bodies of the *golah* themselves.[51] Signaled by the phrase "and because of all of this,"[52] the chapter opens as the priestly response to this "great distress." The swearing of an oath opening Nehemiah 10 calls the people to confront this great distress. Listing Nehemiah's name first, the document gives the names of the priests, the Levites, leaders, gatekeepers, singers, temple slaves, and all who have separated themselves from the peoples of the lands. The listing goes even further by including their wives, daughters, and sons.[53] Usually these subordinate members of the family unit would not be named explicitly, but in this instance precisely they are the subject of this legislation.[54] Immediately after listing the participants, the oath

---

[50] 9:37 English.

[51] But see Manfred Oeming for a positive interpretation of Neh. 9 ("'See, We Are Serving Today' [Nehemiah 9:36]: Nehemiah as a Theological Interpretation of the Persian Period," in *Judah and Judeans in the Persian Period* [ed. Oded Lipschits and Manfred Oeming; Winona Lake, In.: Eisenbrauns, 2006]).

[52] Neh 9:38 English.

[53] Oeming, "See, We Are," 314.

[54] The nature of the marriages and/or divorces is beyond the purview of this study. One particularly erudite inquiry into the subject is the study by Willa Mathis Johnson, "The Holy Seed Has Been Defiled: The Inter-ethnic Marriage Dilemma in Ezra 9-10" (Ph.D. diss., Vanderbilt University, 1999). Johnson focuses on questions concerning psychic effect of exile on a minority population

becomes more emphatic and binding, calling the people to join in a curse invoking the oath's enforcement by a cultural system of shame and honor. As if this were not enough to ensure compliance, the oath is framed as the law of God as given through Moses.[55] In so doing, the rhetoric associates the current priesthood in Jerusalem with the authority of the ancient liberator and with his stature as the lawgiver in the historical consciousness of the people. The rhetoric leaves no questions about either the seriousness with which the priesthood perceives the problem or the urgency with which they call the people to respond.

Finally, there is the first provision of the oath. How does the rhetoric intend the *golah* to respond to this "great distress?" Immediately following the signatories and the preamble communicating the oath's binding nature, Neh 10:30 gives the provisions of the communal oath. Its first provision reads, "We will not give our daughters to the peoples of the lands, nor will we take their daughters for our sons." By juxtaposing it to legislation concerning tithing in the following provision in verse 33,[56] the rhetoric makes clear the connection between preserving group wealth and the ability to support the monetary needs of the temple. In doing so, the rhetoric reveals explicit concerns about preserving the collective wealth of the *golah.*

After a brief mention of the violation of the Sabbath, the text lists the forms in which the funds are to be brought to the temple. On its face, this "commandment/obligation" in verse 33 is intended to fund temple functionaries and temple rituals. This list of tithes recalls some of the "priestly" traditions of the tithe found in the Pentateuch. For the audience, it associates the support of this temple with support of the

---

and intermarriage as a strategy for cultural ascendancy. See also Cheryl B. Anderson, "Reflections in an Interethnic/racial Ear on Interethnic/racial Marriage in Ezra," in *They Were All Together In One Place? Toward Minority Biblical Criticism*, ed. Randall C. Bailey, Tat-siong Benny Liew, and Fernando F. Segovia (Atlanta: Society of Biblical Literature, 2009).

[55] Nehemiah 10:30 reads, "to join with their kin, their nobles, and enter into a curse and an oath to walk in God's law, which was given by Moses the servant of God, and to observe and do all the commandments of the LORD our Lord and his ordinances and his statutes."

[56] Neh 10:32 in English.

Solomonic temple. Through this association, the act of paying the tribute is couched as a continuation of an ancient ancestral tradition.

At the top of the list is silver—one-third of a shekel—required annually from each household. This obligatory one-third shekel recalled the older tax of one-half shekel instituted by Moses for the support of the sanctuary and as a ransom to prevent the onset of any plague.[57] The former tax acted as preventative against the recurrence of the devastating plagues sent upon Egypt. Similarly, looming large behind this new tax is the devastation of the Babylonian exile and the mandate to obey the priesthood so as to prevent any future tragedy. Silver coinage in Yehud was very rare; a full-monied economy would not come about until the Hellenistic period. Placing silver at the top of the list emphasized all the more the urgency of the needs of the distressed temple. Perhaps the temple faced the same imperial requests as those that bankrupted the temple at Uruk in Babylonia. The remainder of the list—the bread, the regular grain offering, the sin offering, and the first fruits collectd by the Levites—replicates the imperial tribute that the Persians required from Babylonian temples. In 10:37, there is a list of grain, wine, and oil that the Levites must bring to the storehouses of the temple. The commodities mentioned here are exactly those that imperial authorities required Babylonian temples to send to royal estates and to imperial officials at the order of the satrap of Ebr Nahara. All of these signify the fiscal needs of the temple.

Since the text states the problem "great distress" (Neh 9:37), as the people's complaint against Persian control of their economic surplus, one would expect that this oath, the priesthood's rhetorical response, to address exactly that. Yet the response—separation from the 'am ha'aretz, Sabbath observance, and tithing—focuses instead on the temple, its rituals, and its needs. Instead of serving to replenish that which Persia has taken from the golah, the response depletes the people's resources even further. This time, however, instead of wealth being seized from the people for the empire, the people are persuaded to give their wealth to the temple. At the very least, there is a rhetorical disconnect, or maybe a rhetorical sleight of hand, where the people's distress is voiced in 9:36-37, but the remedy in chapter 10 satisfies the

---

[57] Ex 30:11-16.

temple's needs. As if to clarify this disconnect, the oath concludes in 10:39 with the simple affirmation, "We will not neglect the house of our God." There is no confusion in the intention of the rhetoric. It is meant to support the "*house of our God*" against the "great distress," that is, Persian taxation of the economic surpluses of the temple.

The divorce rhetoric of chapter 13 is a more emphatic presentation of the same rhetoric in chapter 10. It re-presents the three provisions of the oath as violations of the law that the people of Judah committed. Eliashib has neglected the temple by allowing Tobiah to reside in one of the storerooms (13:4-5), Judahites are transacting with foreign merchants on the Sabbath (13:15-22), and once again intermarriage has polluted the holy seed (13:22-31).

Reiterating the concern over intermarriage emphasizes the urgency of the problem. In 13:23, Nehemiah is disturbed that as a result of the intermarriage that has taken place in Jerusalem, half of the children no longer speak the language of Judah but speak instead the foreign language of their mothers. These children may have been captivated by the allure of the wealth of this landed gentry class and so have chosen the languages and cultures of their more affluent maternal families.[58] Could the Second Temple rely upon these sons, who would inherit their fathers' land, to adhere to the dictates of Mosaic Law by supporting the temple as had their fathers? If not, the temple community faced even further economic hardship. It is no wonder that in verse 25 we read a rapid succession of verbs portraying Nehemiah's active engagement with the exogamists. Nehemiah contends with them, then beats them and pulls out their hair. His work here is no longer legislative

---

[58] See also Daniel L. Smith-Christopher whose work has been helpful in understanding the motivations for instances of hypergamy in Yehud in "The Politics of Ezra: Sociological Indicators of Postexilic Judaean Society," in *Second Temple Studies I: Persian Period* (ed. Philip R. Davies; JSOTS 117 (Sheffield: Sheffield Academic Press, 1991), 82-3. Recently, his argument, which relies upon Merton's structural-functional assumptions, has been updated by Katherine Southwood's discussions of interrelated endogamous boundaries. Katherine Southwood, "The Holy Seed: The Significance of Endogamous Boundaries," in *Judah and Judeans in the Achaemenid Period* (ed. Oded Lipschits, Gary N. Knoppers, and Manfred Oeming; Winona Lake, In.: Eisenbrauns, 2011).

as in chapter 10; it is "hands on," so to speak. It is no longer resigned to using ancient traditions to persuade the *golah* to comply; rather, it is active. In this statement, the rhetoric resorts to the only means of physical enforcement at the priesthood's disposal; it conjures an image of power in the form of violence, directed against the transgressors by the real authority of the province, Nehemiah, cast as a Persian governor.[59]

As instances of intermarriage among the Jerusalem aristocracy increased, the balance of cultural markers exchanged between the Second Temple community and those groups whom it constructed as the *'am ha'arets* flowed away from the Second Temple community. Cultural identity and group cohesion slowly began to erode. The net effect of intermarriage eroded the collective's wealth. Demographically, these unions diminished the number of adherents to the temple. With each instance of intermarriage, the Second Temple priesthood saw the collective's land base and likewise its own potential revenue and ability to meet the imperial tax levy diminish.[60]

Situating the Second Temple Priesthood in Jerusalem: Stratified Interests

In the political economy of Persian Yehud, the Second Temple priesthood, like its counterparts throughout the empire, was a highly stratified group. Within any priesthood throughout the imperial system, priests may be located among the aristocracy, the peasantry, or have

---

[59] Even Nehemiah's legitimacy as an arbiter of orthodoxy was not recognized by some leaders in Jerusalem. This image of Nehemiah weilding imperial power simultaneously evidences resistance to his reforms. For a discussion of the ambiguities of orthodoxy and authority in Yehud, see Gary N. Knoppers, "Revisiting the Samaritan Question in the Persian Period," in *Judah and Judeans in the Persian Period* (ed. Oded Lipschits and Manfred Oeming; Winona Lake, In.: Eisenbrauns, 2006), 279-80.

[60] It is precisely because of the economic concerns of the Second Temple priesthood that I agree with Eskanzi's conclusion that Nehemiah's reforms intended an inclusive posture rather than an exclusive one. Shrinking the collective base or instituting a patently exclusionary policy was counterintuitive to the community's survival. T. C. Eskenazi, "The Missions of Ezra and Nehemiah," in *Judah and Judeans in the Persian Period*, (ed. Oded Lipschits and Manfred Oeming; Winona Lake, In.: Eisenbrauns, 2006).

affinities with both classes. Tenure to arable land and access to temple revenues separated them by class.[61] Priests among the aristocracy leveraged their land tenure as a source of income.[62] These were wealthier

---

[61] Kautsky, *The Politics of Aristocratic Empires*, 161-66. See also Lenski, *Power and Privilege: A Theory of Social Stratification*, 178-79, 257-59. At the beginning of his *Politics,* Kautsky makes two terse but provocative statements. The first is "Peasants are born and die, they sow and they reap, and they labor and pay taxes" and the second is, "Aristocrats, too, are born and die, but they do not sow or reap, they do not labor or pay taxes" (Kautsky, *The Politics of Aristocratic Empires*, 3). He argues further, "their privileges consist in a title of nobility, freedom from taxation, and special rights associated with the control of land. Aristocrats also constitute a hierarchy of honor in which different degrees or ranks are marked by special insignia, the right to bear arms, and the preemption of activities that are believed to confer prestige.... Aristocratic privileges and conventions help to define the circle of those considered eligible for marriage and social intercourse." In these two statements Kautsky draws the simple but stark distinction between the aristocracy and the peasantry. Aristocrats are identified by wealth and prestige only. In other words, aristocrats are defined solely in terms of the economic and political roles they play in society and may overlap with peasants within other groupings (Kautsky, *The Politics of Aristocratic Empires*, 79).

[62] Chief among the sources for aristocratic wealth is tenure to arable land. However, this does not mean that they always owned the land. Even where peasants retained ownership rights to land, they were taxed by the elite, who claimed anywhere from 30 to 70 percent of their crop. The aristocracy also taxed any transfer of land ownership, whether by purchase or inheritance. See Lenski, *Power and Privilege*, 267-70. See particularly his use of Yosoburo Takekoshi, *The Economic Aspects of the History of the Civilization of Japan* (vol. 3; New York: Macmillan Press, 1930), 415. Since the basis of wealth in an agrarian society is land, the aristocracy comprises those who possess the right, given by the ruler or ruling class, to share in the land's economic surplus, produced by the general population. Lenski, *Power and Privilege: A Theory of Social Stratification*, 220. Kautsky explains further that they are those who, without engaging in the work of agricultural labor, consume the produce of the land, appropriating the surplus from peasants' labor for their own purposes (Kautsky, *The Politics of Aristocratic Empires*, 80-81). Aristocrats may also extract funds by taking tribute through various and innovative modes of taxation of peasants and by engaging in the trafficking of enslaved persons. Kautsky emphasizes,

priests who owned land and exploited their resources. On the whole, priesthoods in Egypt and Babylon did not engage in agricultural labor to acquire wealth.[63] Rather, their temple complexes owned vast tracts of land. In Babylon, contracts show that these temples leased land to others for cultivation. Rent from these leases provided operating income for temples. In some instances, the temples complexes also owned enslaved persons, who cultivated the land. Surpluses from their labor enriched the temple economy and subsequently its priesthood. There were also members within the same priesthood whose position in the political economy was determined more by their exploitation as labor than their relationship to natural resources which had more affinities with the peasantry.[64] As Persia intensified its program of extraction, priests with more modest means returned to agrarian labor. There are reports of Egyptian priests having to raise their own produce for sacrifices. These reports comport with the description in Neh 13, where Nehemiah finds

---

however, that these alternative means of gaining wealth are exceptions to the rule. But see Lenski, *Power and Privilege*, 267-70.

[63] In both Egypt and Babylon, their respective pre-Persian monarchs donated to them, and their surrounding community tithed to them. After the advent of Persian domination, the crown ceased tithing to temples. While larger, more influential temples benefitted from the financial largesse of the Persian monarch, the majority of temples suffered a diminution of income.

[64] The peasantry is defined, not by its relationship to natural resources, but instead by its exploitation as labor and by its relationship to the aristocracy. Kautsky describes the peasant class only in terms of its relationship to the aristocracy. Peasants may even own land, but the aristocracy consumes whatever surplus is produced. According to Kautsky, "Unlike any particular property system, it is the universal aspect of the relationship between peasantry and aristocracy and the very basis of the existence of the aristocracy." He argues further, "Exploitation is indeed the principal and only necessary link between the peasants' societies in their villages and the society of the aristocracy, regardless of who "owns" the land. In all cases, while the peasant produces and consumes, the aristocrat does not produce and yet consumes—and generally consumes far more than the peasant. What the aristocrat consumes must be part of the peasant's product whether it is delivered in the form of labor and services, rent, dues, or taxes" (Kautsky, *The Politics of Aristocratic Empires*, 102; cf. Kautsky, *The Politics of Aristocratic Empires*, 103).

that the Levites' portion of the community's economic surplus has not been given to them, so the Levites return to seeking income from cultivating their own fields.

In land tenure, temple systems behaved like any aristocratic institution. They utilized peasants to cultivate produce, retained what surplus was allowed, while the remainder flowed to imperial treasuries. Their priesthoods comprised a stratified class where some members wielded far more power and privilege than others.[65] Similar to their counterparts throughout the empire, the Second Temple priesthood's interest and behaviors reflected this stratification. Priests with more status and wealth, "the upper clergy" acted upon their interests in a manner more closely aligned with the aristocracy, while "lower clergy," those with less status acted in a manner more closely aligned with the peasantry.[66] The polyvalent nature of the divorce rhetoric in Nehemiah 10 and 13 reveals this stratification, and it is to this that we now turn.

Intra-Class Conflict among the Second Temple Jerusalem Priesthood

The reforms advocated by the upper clergy take the shape of a dominant history, a mimetic doubling of the sovereign history of the Persia crown. However, the lower clergy resists these reforms. Their response gestures toward a second order counter-narrative. Ezra 9:2 claims, "... the officials and leaders have led the way." Understanding the priesthood as a stratified class is helpful in explaining the substantial presence of priests among those who have polluted the holy seed. In Ezra 9–10 and Nehemiah 10 and 13, the divorce rhetoric signifies their stratified interests and loyalties. Their unique position resulted in varying interests within the group. At times actions based upon these interests caused conflict within the priesthood as in the case of the divorce rhetoric. Moreover, the priesthood held in tension competing loyalties to Yahweh and the *golah*, to themselves, and to the imperial authorities.

Since the priesthood was a stratified class, individual members' interests and behaviors can also be differentiated along those lines of

---

[65] Lenski, *Power and Privilege: A Theory of Social Stratification*, 284; Kautsky, *The Politics of Aristocratic Empires*, 161-66, 70.

[66] Lenski, *Power and Privilege: A Theory of Social Stratification*, 258-59.

stratification. The text itself reveals at least some stratification between Levites and priests. Some members of the priesthood, those whom I locate in the upper clergy, would have benefitted greatly from the *teruma*. The interests of these cultic elites would have been intensely invested in maintaining a closed community that retained tenure to the most arable land from which to tithe. This group would have reason to support the separatism of the *golah* more zealously than did other members of the cult, those who benefitted less. Other members of the priesthood, those whom both Lenski and Kautsky describe as more closely associated with the peasantry, may have benefitted less from the *teruma* and would have had more incentive to intermarry, particularly if intermarriage afforded them a greater measure of economic stability.

Eagleton's concept of dominant ideology is helpful in understanding this conflict in interests. "What we call a dominant ideology is typically that of a dominant social bloc, made up of classes and factions whose interests are not always at one; and these compromises and divisions will be reflected in the ideology itself."[67] In Nehemiah 13:10, Nehemiah chastises the priesthood because the Levites have not received their "portion," that is, they have not received their share of the *teruma*. In Ezra 10:15, Jonathan, son of Asahel, and Jahzeiah, son of Tikvah, oppose Ezra's activity and Meshullam, Shabbethai, and the Levites support Jonathan's opposition to Ezra. In this instance, apparently those of the lower clergy, and Levitical priests, who might not have benefitted as much by the receipt of the tithe, opposed the restructuring of the community. The conflict reflects the priesthood's status as a center within the province but as peripheral to the empire. Lower clergy and Levites find themselves marginalized even within priestly ranks. In the end, those members of the priesthood with rank, status, and wealth would have been able to communicate their interests in the prevailing rhetoric and to castigate those in their class whose marital practices were contrary to the interests of the upper clergy. The upper clergy's story predominates in Ezra 9–10 and Nehemiah 10 and 13.

---

[67] Terry Eagleton, *Ideology: An Introduction* (London: Verso, 1991), 45.

Conclusion

Temple economies, which often dominated their locales, were important to imperial fiscal administration. In both Egypt and Babylon, temple inventories included latifundia for which they conscripted laborers. Their officials transformed these human and natural resources into material surpluses. As had their predecessors, the Achaemenids employed an efficient bureaucracy to manage temple personnel and to track, protect, and tax their surpluses. Jerusalem's temple would have faced similar expectations from imperial authorities.

Nehemiah 10 and 13 also discloses the priesthood's precarious socioeconomic position. On one hand, the priesthood was pressed by the empire to meet the fiscal burden placed on the temple in order to satisfy imperial authorities. On the other hand, it had no choice but to work within an already established cultural tradition in order to enjoy legitimation by Mosaic Law. Even within the priesthood, class stratification reveals a mimetic doubling of the sovereign and counter-history dialectic. This second-order dialectic between upper and lower clergy points to the differing interests in the exogamous marriages between the Levites and other members of the priesthood. In the small, poor province, the priesthood had little in the way of material resources to appropriate in the service of cultural maintenance or even to meet the fiscal burdens of imperial rule. They were not, however, content to stand by as their revenue, power, and community diminished. Instead, they resorted to symbolic resources of which they made good use. We find their response in the rhetoric's economic signification. Lines distinguishing tithe to the cult and tribute to the empire blur when they intersect at the maintenance of the temple. The agricultural surpluses that the temple needed from its community consisted of the same products that the empire demanded from any local temple. So the temple itself held multiple significations. It was simultaneously the imperial bureaucratic and financial center of the province and "the house of our God." Most likely constructed at the behest of Darius, whose predecessor Cyrus had already been blessed by Yahweh in Deutero-Isaiah, the temple held the dual significations of royal and religious ideologies. Its priests negotiated this dual signification in a way that preserved their power and authority over the people, lest the imperial authorities remove them, but simultaneously preserved the integrity and existence of the *golah*. The rhetoric reflects this dual signification. In its economic expression, the rhetoric, in effect, does double duty. For the Second Temple community, it is patently theological. It frames for them the creation of a Yahwistic community constructed according to the dictates of Mosaic Law. It calls upon their ancient traditions, laws, and personalities—now long relegated to their collective historical consciousness—and reinscribes them with the contemporary realities of life for the *golah* under Persian domination. It invokes ancient religious traditions, reinterprets their meanings, and calls the people to adhere to them. These new meanings support the activity and ascendancy of the present priesthood and their ability to legislate in favor of financial support to the temple. For the priesthood, the rhetoric is a powerful tool oriented toward meeting the temple's fiscal burdens under imperial policies of depletion while maintaining the community's economic stability.

In sum, in Nehemiah 10 and 13, the rhetoric's economic signification communicates both sovereign and counter-knowledge to negotiate imperial fiscal pressures. Its dominant voice assures the empire that this temple will meet its fiscal obligations no differently than temples throughout the imperial system. Unlike the counter-narrative, the dominant narrative gives no voice to the people's distress as a result of imperial repression. Rather, its response compels the community to commit its labor to support the imperial machine. In order to ensure such support, the priesthood, maintained ethnic boundaries to structure its community toward meeting imperial obligations. Family units that may not be counted upon to contribute to the effort to meet the temple's tax levy found themselves "outside" of the ethnic boundary. Its subversive voice compels the community's performance toward an alternative history based on counter-knowledge, namely a shared culture and identity distinct from their existence as Persian subjects. This alternative history does not attend to the Persian Empire, but rather to supporting the "House of [their] God." Ultimately, it fortifies the community's cultural center and ensures the community's long-term survival.

Chapter 6

Conclusion

This study began with three lines of inquiry: an initial question about the function of the divorce rhetoric in Ezra 9-10 and Neh 10 and 13; a secondary question concerning the social world of Jerusalem during the Persian period; and a methodological concern about whether an ideological critique could control for both the circularity and anachronism that result from using Ezra-Nehemiah to reconstruct the Persian context. In other words, no sufficient analysis of the meanings of the divorce rhetoric of Ezra-Nehemiah could proceed outside of a method adequate to attend to the aesthetic product, the divorce rhetoric, and the material context, the historical world of the Persian period. Although the historical and methodological questions became more prominent as the study progressed, the rhetoric itself and its multiple meanings remained the primary concern.

The already well-developed tradition of ideological criticism in Hebrew Bible studies has shown how struggles for power found within the text represent struggles in the social world of ancient Israel. Nonetheless, ideological criticism as a mode of exegesis continues to challenge scholars to test the text's rhetoric, stories, struggles, and ideologies against a plausible, if not real, historical context—one not constructed solely from the biblical text's stories written long after the periods they describe. Since few sources for such a reconstruction of ancient Israel's social world exist, some studies turn to the biblical text itself as a source. In these instances, the aesthetic product participates in the critic's construct of the material context. The result admits circularity into the process and results in an inevitably anachronistic historical reconstruction. By making no assumption about the historicity of Ezra-

Nehemiah, this study describes a social context of Jerusalem under Persian dominion that relies only minimally upon the description in the Hebrew Bible. The result in the rhetorical analyses tests whether Persian Jerusalem is a plausible site for the emergence of the divorce rhetoric's concerns and how such rhetoric would function if, in fact, it operated in that social context.

Since the divorce rhetoric holds implications for the political, cultic, and economic valences of Jerusalem's social world, the description attends to each in order to give a more fulsome rendering. At each level, Persian administrative policy was consistent across the imperial bureaucracy from Mesopotamia to Egypt, with no exception made for Jerusalem. Rather, Jerusalem, the most important city in the small, poor province of Yehud, was tied into the imperial system as an outpost between Susa and the satrapy of Egypt. In Jerusalem, the priesthood is the most plausible source of the rhetoric. In fact, because the divorce rhetoric is *prima facie* religious in character, scholarly consensus has accepted the position that it stems from some priesthood operating in Jerusalem. The murkier question is the nature of the relationship between the Second Temple priesthood and the Persian imperial bureaucracy. Jerusalem existed in the world dominated by the imperial system whose power shaped the social, political, and economic realities at every level. Understanding the priesthood this way contextualizes their activity within a dynamic web of both external pressures and internal concerns. Taking into account its response to the imperial system renders a balanced portrait of the priesthood.

Traditionally, however, this has not always been the case. Some depictions of the priesthood reduce it to self-interested bureaucrats who operated with disregard for the Second Temple community. These studies ignore both the external realities of imperial domination and the priesthood's real commitments to the Second Temple community. Other portraits of the Second Temple priesthood are plagued by assumptions of religious exceptionalism that exonerate the priesthood from any culpability for abuses of power and repression. These studies emphasize the priesthood's commitment to the Second Temple community but ignore the realities of priesthoods across the ancient Near East.

By contrast, this book models the portrait of the Second Temple priesthood on its counterparts, which operated within the Persian imperial system in both Babylon and Egypt to correct for both types of distortion. The resulting picture is of a Jerusalem priesthood that is no more or no less self-interested than its counterparts in other provinces. Likewise, the Persian authorities treated the cultic center there no differently than they treated other temples throughout the empire. Just as temples in Babylon and Egypt offered the divine legitimacy essential for imperial rule, so also did the Second Temple. Just as temples in Babylon and Egypt acted as an organizing center for the local economy, so also did Jerusalem's temple. Yehud's economic resources, however, were few. Moreover, the community it served was smaller than that of its counterparts in Babylon and Egypt. It produced less than more prominent temples in Egypt and Babylon. Nonetheless, its importance to the empire was in no way diminished by its size. Yehud's importance was its strategically significant locale—on the western frontier of the Persian Empire situated on trade routes to the wealthy and ever politically restless satrapy of Egypt. Most important, Jerusalem's temple, like its counterparts in Egypt and Babylon was subject to the empire's regular practice of taxing temple wealth.

Similar to its counterparts in both Babylon and Egypt, the Second Temple priesthood struggled both to negotiate its existence and to live out an expression of its Yahwistic faith amidst exorbitant taxation and military violence that were all a part of the day-to-day realities of life under imperial dominion. In this position, the Second Temple priesthood accommodated imperial rule when forced to do so and when imperial policies coincided with their interests, and resisted imperial rule when possible or when the degree of the imperial repression threatened its survival or that of the Second Temple community.

This third question regards the polysemic nature of rhetoric and its polyvalent intentionalities in the social world. The book deeply historicizes the divorce rhetoric by grounding it within the social world of Yehud. In that context, its dominant and subversive voices emerge and participate in creating worlds of meaning for both the imperial authorities and the Second Temple community respectively. Within the same rhetoric, the priesthood constructed significations that affirmed the divergent interests of both groups simultaneously. For the empire, the rhetoric's dominant voices coalesced as a sovereign history, while the subversive voice composed coveyed counter-knowledges and, ulitimately, a counterhistory. At the political level, the rhetoric is a discourse between the Jerusalem priesthood and the imperial authorities.

Just as priesthoods in Babylonia and Egypt deployed native religious traditions to affirm Persian rule, the priesthood in Jerusalem deployed its own religious traditions in the same manner. Analogous to pro-Persian religious literature in Babylonia and Egypt, the rhetoric's dominant voice supports the interests of the imperial authorities by encouraging the community to accept Persian imperial rule and to view the Persian king as Yahweh's emissary. Ezra 9:7-9 calls upon the people to accept their current circumstance and encourages them to participate in the Persian program of developing this western frontier of the empire. For the empire, work done by religious ideology supported Persian domination more cost effectively than military intervention. For the Second Temple priesthood, the rhetoric satisfies its imperial benefactor. Both accommodation and resistance make sense as interests of the Second Temple priesthood. Their motives, interests, and desires were as complex and polyvalent as the rhetoric itself. By constructing rhetoric that encouraged the *golah* to accept imperial rule, the Second Temple priesthood demonstrated to imperial authorities its compliance as loyal imperial subjects. Accommodation holds obvious benefits for the Second Temple community. By complying with imperial expectations, the priesthood staved off violent excesses of repression that occurred in both Babylon and Egypt, where Xerxes and Cambyses destroyed local cults and directed acts of violence against their populations. At this level, the rhetoric resisted imperial domination and ensures the survival of the *golah.*

At the cultic level, the priesthood and the Second Temple community participate in a subversive discourse, a counter history. Just as priesthoods in Babylonia and Egypt resisted imperial dominion where feasible, so too did the priesthood of Jerusalem. The rhetoric deploys the symbols of a shared history to remind the Second Temple community that Yahweh's authority trumps that of the empire. Ezra 9–10 vests the temple with divine legitimation symbolizing Yahweh's power rather than imperial dominion. By emphasizing divine legitimacy, the rhetoric masks the cult's imperial origins: the source of funding of the temple's construction, the temple's utility for the empire, and the empire's alliance with the priesthood. Obfuscating these contradictions in the temple's symbolism invited the community to coalesce around shared interests and cultural markers. In effect, the rhetoric called community to work against imperial interests and toward cultural fortification.

At the economic level, all three groups participate in the discourse, albeit at different levels. Its intent is twofold. Its dominant voice enlisted the community's support in raising funds to meet the temple's tax burden in order to demonstrate to imperial authorities the Second Temple priesthood's compliance. In the discourse between the Second Temple priesthood and its Yahwistic community, the divorce rhetoric's subversive intent is cast as a response to the "great distress" of Nehemiah 9, namely, pervasive Persian control over the social world of the *golah,* even the very bodies of the *golah* themselves.

Central to the priesthood's response is the connection between two ideas that are seemingly unrelated to the complaint in Nehemiah 9. The first is the command to separate. The second, juxtaposed against the first, is a legislation concerning tithing. Taken together, both statements connect the financial support of the temple to dissolving exogamous marriages. The commands preserve Jerusalem's economic viability against Persian taxation. Although the rhetoric voices the people's distress, the net effect does not lessen the imperial tax burden upon the people, but reframes it as an obligation to the temple. In fact, the priesthood had no power to affect imperial tax policy. The rhetoric intends such a connection where ultimately the priesthood and its community understood that their identity and interests fully coincided with the interests and survival of the temple.

Finally, the divorce rhetoric of Ezra-Nehemiah, the priesthood's response to the stark and brutal realities of imperial domination, reveals a social world of competing and cooperating groups with diverse and complex interests. Its effects, as polyvalent as the rhetoric itself, both accommodate and resist imperial repression. The commands land with brutal force on the lives of the Second Temple community and exacerbated an already strained economy. The trauma caused by the arbitrary construction of ethnic boundaries and the dissolution of marriages is too horrific to imagine. Nonetheless, against a world dominated by imperial repression, the rhetoric, a counter-history, hewed a space for cultural survival and galvanized the community around its cultural symbols and shared history to create an enduring identity among its members. Fortified by tributes that satisfied imperial demands, the temple complex and the Second Temple community survived the shrinking imperial economy and its increasingly repressive policies, and ultimately outlived the Persian Empire itself.

Bibliography

Ackroyd, Peter R. "Archaeology, Politics, and Religion: The Persian Period." *The Iliff Review* 39 (1982): 5-24.

_____. *Exile and Restoration: A Study of Hebrew Thought of the Sixth Century B.C*, The Old Testament library. Philadelphia: Westminster Press, 1968.

_____. *I & II Chronicles, Ezra, Nehemiah*. London: SCM Press, 1973.

_____, ed. *Israel under Babylon and Persia*. Repr. with corrections. The New Clarendon Bible. Old Testament; v. 4. Oxford, [Oxfordshire]; New York: Oxford University Press, 1979.

Ahlström, Gösta. *The History of Ancient Palestine*. Minneapolis: Fortress Press, 1994.

Albertz, Rainer. *A History of Israelite Religion in the Old Testament Period*. Old Testament Library. Louisville, Ky: Westminster John Knox Press, 1994.

_____. "The Controversy About Judean Versus Israelite Identity." Pages 483-504 in *Judah and Judeans in the Achaemenid Period*, edited by Oded Lipschits, Gary N. Knoppers and Manfred Oeming. Winona Lake, In.: Eisenbrauns, 2011.

Alt, Albrecht. "Die Rolle Samarias bei der Entstehung des Judentums." Pages 316-37 in *Kleine Schriften ur Geschichte des Volkes Israel, II*. Munich: Beck, 1953.

_____. "Die Rolle Samarias bei der Entstehung des Judentums." Pages 5-28 in *Fetstschrift Otto Procksch zum sechzigsten Geburtstag*. Edited by Albrecht Alt et al. Leipzig: J. C. Hinrichs, 1934.

Anderson, Cheryl B. *Women, Ideology and Violence: Critical Theory and the Construction of Gender in the Book of the Covenant and the Deuteronomic Law*. New York: Continuum, 2004.

_____. "Reflections in an Interethnic/Racial Ear on Interethnic/ Racial Marriage in Ezra." In *They Were All Together in One Place?: Toward Minority Biblical Criticism*, edited by Randall C. Bailey, Tat-siong Benny Liew and Fernando F. Segovia. 47-64. Atlanta: Society of Biblical Literature, 2009.

Azzoni, Annalisa. "Women and Property in Persian Egypt and Mesopotamia." Paper presented at the Colloquium on Women and Property in Ancient Near Eastern and Mediterranean Societies, The Center for Hellenic Studies-Harvard University, 2002.

Bailey, Randall C. "Beyond Identification: The Use of Africans in Old Testament Poetry and Narratives." In *Stony the Road We Trod: African American Biblical Interpretation*. Edited by Cain Hope Felder. Minneapolis: Fortress Press, 1991.

_____. "They're Nothing but Incestuous Bastards: The Polemical Use of Sex and Sexuality in Hebrew Canon Narratives." Pages 121-38 in *Reading from This Place: Social Location and Biblical Interpretation in the United States*. Edited by Fernando F. Segovia and Mary Ann Tolbert. Minneapolis: Fortress Press, 1995.

_____. "The Danger of Ignoring One's Own Cultural Bias." In *The Postcolonial Bible,* edited by R. S. Sugirtharajah. Sheffield: Sheffield Academic Press, 1998.

Beaulieu, Paul-Alain. *The Reign of Nabonidus: King of Babylon 556-539 B.C.* New Haven: Yale University Press, 1989.

Bedford, Peter R. "On Models and Texts: A Response To Blenkinsopp and Petersen." in *Second Temple Studies I: Persian Period*.

Edited by Philip R. Davies. JSOTSup 117. Edited by Philip R. Davies. Sheffield: Sheffield Academic Press, 1991.

Becking, Bob. ""We All Returned as One!": Critical Notes on the Myth of the Mass Return." Pages 3-18 in *Judah and the Judeans in the Persian Period*. Edited by Oded Lipschits and Manfred Oeming. Winona Lake, In.: Eisenbrauns, 2006.

Berquist, Jon. *Judaism in Persia's Shadow: A Social and Historical Approach*. Minneapolis: Fortress Press, 1995.

_____. "Constructions of Identity in Postcolonial Yehud." Pages 53-66 in *Judah and the Judeans in the Persian Period*. Edited by Oded Lipschits and Manfred Oeming. Winona Lake, In.: Eisenbrauns, 2006.

Bickerman, E. J. "The Edict of Cyrus in Ezra 1." *Journal of Biblical Literature* 65 (1946): 249-75.

Birch, Bruce C. *Let Justice Roll Down: The Old Testament, Ethics, and Christian life*. 1st ed. Louisville, Ky.: Westminster John Knox Press, 1991.

Bird, Phyllis. *Missing Persons and Mistaken Identities: Women and Gender in Ancient Israel*, Overtures to Biblical Theology. Minneapolis: Fortress Press, 1997.

Blenkinsopp, J. "The Mission of Udjahorresnet and Those of Ezra and Nehemiah." *Journal of Biblical Literature* 106 (1987): 409-21.

_____. *Ezra-Nehemiah*. Edited by Peter Ackroyd, The Old Testament Library. Philadelphia: Westminster Press, 1988.

_____. "Temple and Society in Achaemenid Judah." in *Second Temple Studies: 1. Persian Period*. Edited by Philip R. Davies. JSOTSup 117. Sheffield: Sheffield Academic Press, 1991.

Bresciani, E. "The Persian Occupation of Egypt." Pages 502-28 in *The Cambridge History of Iran: Volume 2 The Median and Achaemenian Periods*. Edited by Ilya Gerschevitch. New York: Cambridge University Press, 1985.

Briant, Pierre. *From Cyrus to Alexander: A History of the Persian Empire*. Translated by Peter T. Daniels. Winona Lake, Indiana: Eisenbrauns, 2002.

Bright, John. "The Date of the Prose Sermons in Jeremiah." *Journal of Biblical Literature* 70 (1951).

Broshi, M. and I. Finkelstein. "The Population of Palestine in Iron Age II." *BASOR* 287 (1992): 46-70.

Cameron, George Glenn. *Persepolis Treasure Tablets*. Vol. 65, University of Chicago Oriental Institute Publications. Chicago: University of Chicago Press, 1948.

Camp, Claudia V. "The Female Sage in Ancient Israel and in the Biblical Wisdom Literature." Pages 185-203 in *The Sage in Israel and the Ancient Near East*. Edited by John G. Gammie and Leo G. Perdue. Winona Lake, In: Eisenbrauns, 1990.

Carroll, Robert P. "The Myth of the Empty Land." *Semeia* 59 (1992): 79-91.

Carter, Charles E. *The Emergence of Yehud in the Persian Period: A Social and Demographic Study*. Sheffield: Sheffield Academic Press, 1999.

Clay, A. T. *Business Documents of Murashû*. Vol. 2 p.1. Publications of the Babylonian Section. Philadelphia: University of Pennsylvania, 1912.

Clines, David J. A. *Ezra, Nehemiah, Esther: Based on the Revised Standard Version*. New Century Bible Commentary. Grand Rapids: Eerdmans, 1984.

Cook, J.M. "The Rise of the Achaemenids and Establishment of Their Empire." Pages 200-91 in *The Cambridge History of Iran: Volume 2 The Median and Achaemenian Periods*. Edited by Ilya Gerschevitch. New York: Cambridge University Press, 1985.

Copher, Charles B. "The Black Presence in the Old Testament." Pages 144-64 in *Stony the Road We Trod : African American Biblical Interpretation*, edited by Cain Hope Felder. Minneapolis, Minn.: Fortress Press, 1991.

Cowley, A. E. *Aramaic Papyri of the Fifth Century B.C.* Oxford: Oxford University Press, 1923.

Dandamaev, M. A., Vladimir Grigor evich Lukonin, Philip L. Kohl, and D. J. Dadson. *The Culture and Social Institutions of Ancient Iran.* Cambridge; New York: Cambridge University Press, 1989.

Dandamaev, M. A. "The Domain-Lands of Achaemenes in Babylonia." *Altorientalische Forschungen* 1 (1974).

_____. *Slavery in Babylonia from Nabopolassar to Alexander the Great (626-331 B.C.)*: Northern Illinois University Press, 1984.

_____. "Neo-Babylonian Society and Economy." Pages 252-75 in *The Cambridge Ancient History: The Assyrian and Babylonian Empires and Other States of the Near East, from the Eighth to the Sixth Centuries B.C.* Edited by John Boardman, I.E.S. Edwards, et al. New York: Cambridge University Press, 1991.

_____. "Achaemenid Babylonia." Pages 296-311 in *Ancient Mesopotamia: A Collection of Studies by Soviet Scholars.* Edited by I.M. Diakonoff. Moscow: Nauka Publishing House, 1969.

_____. *Iranians in Achaemenid Babylonia.* Edited by Ehsan Yarshater. Vol. 6, Columbia Lectures on Iranian Studies. New York: Mazda Publishers, 1992.

Davies, Philip R. *In Search of 'Ancient Israel'.* Journal for the Study of the Old Testament Supplement Series 148. Sheffield: Sheffield Academic Press, 1992.

Dor, Yonina. "The Rite of Separation of the Foreign Wives in Ezra-Nehemiah." Pages 173-88 in *Judah and Judeans in the Achaemenid Period.* Edited by Oded Lipschits, Gary N. Knoppers and Manfred Oeming. Winona Lake, In.: Eisenbrauns, 2011.

Durkheim, Emile. *Elementary Forms of Religious Life.* Translated by Karen Elise Fields. New York: Free Press, 1995.

Eagleton, Terry. *Criticism and Ideology.* 3rd ed. London: Verso, 1982.

_____. *Ideology: An Introduction.* London: Verso, 1991.

Edelman, Diana. *The Origins of the 'Second' Temple: Persian Imperial Policy and the Rebuilding of Jerusalem*. London: Equinox, 2005.

Eichorn, Johann Gottfried. *Einleitung ins Alte Testament*. Leipzig: Weidmanns Erben und Reich, 1787.

Eisenstadt, S. N. *The Political Systems of Empires: The Rise and Fall of Historical Bureaucratic Societies*. New York: Free Press, 1969.

Eliade, Mircea. *The Sacred and the Profane: The Nature of Religion*. Translated by Willard R. Trask,. Harvest book. New York: Harcourt Brace Jovanovich, 1987.

Eskenazi, T. C. *In an Age of Prose: A Literary Approach to Ezra-Nehemiah*. Society of Biblical Literature Monograph Series 36. Atlanta: Scholars Press, 1988.

_____. "The Missions of Ezra and Nehemiah." Pages 509-30 in *Judah and Judeans in the Persian Period*. Edited by Oded Lipschits and Manfred Oeming. Winona Lake, In.: Eisenbrauns, 2006.

Eskenazi, T.C. and Eleanore P. Judd. "Marriage to a Stranger in Ezra 9-10." Pages 266-85 in *Second Temple Studies II: Temple and Community in the Persian Period*. Edited by T.C. Eskenazi and Kent H. Richards. Sheffield: Sheffield Academic Press, 1994.

Fontaine, Carole R. "The Social Roles of Women in the World of Wisdom." In *A Feminist Companion to Wisdom Literature*. Edited by Athalya Brenner. Sheffield: Sheffield Academic Press, 1995.

Frei, Peter and Klaus Koch. *Reichsidee und Reichorganisation im Perserreich*. 2nd ed, Orbis biblicus et orientalus 55. Fribourg: Universitätverlag, 1996.

Fried, Lisbeth S. *The Priest and the Great King: Temple-Palace Relations in the Persian Empire*. Winona Lake, In.: Eisenbrauns, 2004

_____. "The 'Am Ha'ares in Ezra 4:4 and Persian Imperial Administration." Pages 123-46 In *Judah and Judeans in the Persian Period*. Edited by Oded Lipschits and Manfred Oeming.

Winona Lake, In.: Eisenbrauns, 2006.

Michel Foucault, *The History of Sexuality Volume 1: An Introduction.* New York: Vintage Books, 1990.

_____. *"Society Must Be Defended": Lectures at the Collège de France. 1975-1976.* Translated by David Macy. New York: Picador, 2003.

Galling, Kurt. "Bagoas und Ezra." Pages 149-84 in *Studien zur Geschichte Israels im Persischen Zeitalter.* Tübingen: Mohr, 1964.

Geertz, Clifford. *The Interpretation of Cultures.* New York: Basic Books, 1973.

Geuss, Raymond. *The Idea of a Critical Theory: Habermas and the Frankfurt School.* New York: Cambridge University Press, 1988.

Gorman, Frank H. *The Ideology of Ritual: Space, Time, and Status in the Priestly Theology.* Edited by David J. A. Clines, JSOTSup 91. Sheffield: Sheffield Academic Press, 1990.

Gottwald, Norman K. *The Hebrew Bible: A Socio-literary Introduction.* Philadelphia: Fortress Press, 1985.

_____. *The Tribes of Yahweh: A Sociology of the Religion of Liberated Israel 1250-1050 B.C.E.* Maryknoll, NY: Orbis Books, 1979.

_____. "Sociology." Pages 79-89 in *Anchor Bible Dictionary.* Edited by David Noel Freedman. New York: Doubleday, 1992.

Grabbe, Lester L. *Ezra-Nehemiah.* New York: Routledge, 1998.

_____. *Judaism from Cyrus to Hadrian I. The Persian and Greek Periods.* Minneapolis: Fortress Press, 1992.

_____. "The Law of Moses and the Ezra Tradition: More Virtual Than Real?" Pages 91-113 in *Persia and Tora: The Theory of Imperial Authorization of the Pentateuch.* Edited by James L. Watts. Vol. 17 of *SBL Symposium Series.* Atlanta: Society of Biblical Literature, 2001.

_____. "The Persian Documents in the Book of Ezra: Are They Authentic?" Pages 531-70 in *Judah and Judeans in the Persian Period*, edited by Oded Lipschits and Manfred Oeming. Winona Lake, In.: Eisenbrauns, 2006.

Grayson, Albert Kirk. *Assyrian and Babylonian Chronicles*. Winona Lake, In.: Eisenbrauns, 2000.

Habermas, Jürgen *Legitimation Crisis*. Translated by Thomas McCarthy. Boston: Beacon Press, 1975.

Habermas, Jürgen and Niklas Luhmann, *Theorie der Gesellschaft oder Sozialtechnologie. Was leistet die Systemforschung?* Frankfurt: Suhrkamp, 1971.

Halévy, Joseph. "Esdras a-t-il promulgué une loi nouvelle?" *Revue de l'Histoire des Religions* XII (1885): 26-58.

_____. "Esdras et le code Sacerdotal." *Revue de l'Histoire des Religions* IV (1881): 22-45.

Hallock, R. T. "The Evidence of the Persepolis Tablets." Pages 588-609 in *The Cambridge History of Iran: The Median and Achaemenian Periods*. Edited by Ilya Gershevitch. New York: Cambridge University Press, 1985.

Hanson, P.D. *Dawn of the Apocalyptic*. Philadelphia: Westminster, 1973.

Herodotus. *The History*. Translated by David Greene. Chicago: University of Chicago Press, 1987.

Hoglund, Kenneth. *Achaemenid Administration in Syria-Palestine and the Missions of Ezra and Nehemiah*. SBLDS125. Atlanta: Scholars Press, 1992.

_____. "The Achaemenid Context." Pages 54-68 in *Second Temple Studies 1:Persian Period*. Edited by Philip R. Davies. JSOTSup 117. Sheffield: Sheffield Academic Press, 1991.

Hoonacker, Albin van. "Néhémie et Esdras." *Le Muséon* IX (1890): 151-84, 317-51, 89-401.

Hunt, Alice. *Missing Priests: The Zadokites in Tradition and History*. New York: T&T Clark, 2006.

Japhet, Sara. "Periodization between History and Ideology II:
    Chronology and Ideology in Ezra-Nehemiah." Pages 491-508 in
    Judah and Judeans in the Persian Period. Edited by Oded
    Lipschits and Manfred Oeming. Winona Lake, In.: Eisenbrauns,
    2006.

Johnson, Willa Mathis. "The Holy Seed Has Been Defiled: The Inter-
    ethnic Marriage Dilemma in Ezra 9-10." Ph.D. dissertation,
    Vanderbilt University, 1999.

Kautsky, John H. *The Politics of Aristocratic Empires.* 2nd ed. New
    Brunswick, N.J.: Transaction Publishers, 1997.

Kellerman, U. *Nehemia: Quellen Überlieferung und Geschichte*, BZAW
    102. Berlin, 1967.

Knight, Douglas A. "Wellhausen and the Interpretation of Israel's
    Literature." *Semeia* 25 (1982).

Knoppers, Gary N. "Revisiting the Samaritan Question in the Persian
    Period." Pages 189-224 in *Judah and Judeans in the Persian
    Period.* Edited by Oded Lipschits and Manfred Oeming. Winona
    Lake, In.: Eisenbrauns, 2006.

Koch, Klaus. "Ezra and the Origins of Judaism." *Journal of Semetic
    Studies* (1974): 173-97.

Kosters, W.H. *Die Wiederherstellung Israels in der persischen Periode.*
    Translated by A. Basedow. Heidelberg: Hörning, 1895.

Kritzman, Lawrence D., ed. *Politics, Philosphy, Culture: Interviews and
    Other Writings of Michel Foucault 1977-1984.* New York:
    Routledge, 1990.

Kuenen, Abraham. *Gesammelte Abhandlungen zur biblischen
    Wissenschaft von Abraham Kuenen.* Freiburg: J. C. B. Mohr,
    1894.

_____. "L'oevre d'Esdras." *Revue de l'Histoire des Religions* XIII
    (1886): 334-58.

Kuhrt, Amelie. *The Ancient Near East c. 3000-330 BC.* Edited by Fergus
    Millar. 2 vols. Vol. 1, Routledge History of the Ancient World.
    New York: Routledge, 1995.

Kuhrt, Amélie. "The Cyrus Cylinder and Achaemenid Imperial Policy."
    Journal for the Study of the Old Testament 25 (1983): 83-97.

_____. *The Persian Empire: A Corpus of Sources from the
    Achaemenid Period*. 2 vols. Vol. 2, 2007.

Khurt, Amélie and Susan Sherwin-White. "Xerxes' Destruction of
    Babylonian Temples." Pages 70-78 in *Achaemenid History II:
    The Greek Sources*. Edited by Heleen Sancisi-Weerdenburg and
    Amélie Khurt. Leiden: Nederlands Instituut Voor Het Nabije
    Oosten, 1987.

Lemche, Neils Peter. *Ancient Israel: A New History of Israelite Society*.
    Sheffield: Sheffield Academic Press, 1995.

Lenski, G. E. *Power and Privilege: A Theory of Social Stratification*.
    Chapel Hill: University of North Carolina Press, 1984.

Lichtheim, Miriam. Ancient Egyptian Literature. Vol. 3. Berkeley and
    Los Angeles: University of California Press, 1980.

Lipschits, Oded. "Demographic Changes in Judah between the Seventh
    and Fifth Centuries B.C.E." Pages 323-376 in *Judah and
    Judeans in the Neo-Babylonian*. Edited by Oded Lipschits and
    Joseph Blenkensopp. Winona Lake, In.: Eisenbrauns, 2003.

_____. *The Fall and Rise of Jerusalem: The History of Judah
    under Babylonian Rule*. Winona Lake, In.: Eisenbrauns, 2005.

_____. "Achaemenid Imperial Policy, Settlement Processes in
    Palestine and the Status of Jerulalem in the Middle of the Fifth
    Century B.C.E." Pages 19-52 in *Judah and Judeans in the
    Persian Period*. Edited by Oded Lipschits and Manfred Oeming.
    Winona Lake, In.: Eisenbrauns, 2006.

Lundquist, John M. "What is a Temple? A Preliminary Typology." Pages
    205-19 in *The Quest for the Kingdom of God: Studies in Honor
    of George E. Mendenhall*. Edited by H.B. Huffmon, F. A. Spina,
    and A. R. W. Green. Winona Lake, IN: Eisenbrauns, 1983.

Machinist, Peter. "The First Coins of Judah and Samaria: Numismatics
    and History in the Achaemenid and Early Hellenistic Periods."
    Pages 365-80 in *Achaemenid History VIII*. Edited by A. Kuhrt

and M. Cool Root. Leiden: Nederlands Instituut Voor Het Nabije Oosten, 1994.

Marbury, Herbert Robinson. "Ezra-Nehemiah." Pages 280-85 in *The Africana Bible: Reading Israel's Scriptures from Africa and the African Diaspora*. Edited by Hugh R. Page, et al. Minneapolis: Fortress Press, 2010.

Martin, Cary J. "The Demotic Texts." In *The Elephantine Papyri in English: Three Millennia of Cross-Cultural Continuity and Change*. Edited by Belazel Porten. New York: E.J. Brill, 1996.

McEwan, G. J. P. *The Late Babylonian Tablets in the Royal Ontario Museum*. Vol. 2, Royal Ontario Museum Cuneiform Texts. Toronto, 1982.

Meeks, Dimitri. "Les donations aux temples dans l'Égypte du Ier millénaire avant J.-C." in *State and Temple Economy in the Ancient Near East*. Edited by E. Lipinski. Louvain: Departement Orientalistiek, 1979.

Meshorer, Y. *Ancient Jewish Coinage I. Persian Period through Hasmonaeans*. Dix Hills, NY: Amphora Books, 1982.

Meyers, Carol. "Discovering Eve: Ancient Israelite Women in Context." New York: Oxford University Press, 1988.

Meyers, Jacob. *Ezra Nehemiah*. Edited by William Foxwell Albright and David Noel Freedman, The Anchor Bible. New York: Doubleday, 1965.

Michaelis, J. D. *Üebersetzung des Alten Testaments mit Anmerkungun für Ungelehrte*. Göttingen: J. C. Dieterich, 1785.

Mildenberg, L. "On the Money Circulation in Palestine from Artaxerxes II till Ptolemy I: Preliminary Studies of Local Coinage in the Fifth Persian Satrapy. Part 5." *Transeuphratène* 7 (1994): 63-71.

Miller, J. Maxwell and John Haralson Hayes. *A History of Ancient Israel and Judah*. 1st ed. Philadelphia: Westminster Press, 1986.

Morganstern, Julian. "A Chapter in the History of the High Priesthood—Concluded." *American Journal of Semitic Languages and Literature* 55 (1938): 360-77.

_____. "The Dates of Ezra and Nehemiah." *Journal of Semetic Studies* 7 (1962): 1-11.

_____. "Jerusalem—456 B.C." *HUCA* 27 (1956): 101-70.

_____. "Jerusalem—456 B.C. (concluded)." *HUCA* 31 (1960): 1-29.

_____. "Jerusalem—456 B.C., cont." *HUCA* 28 (1957): 15-47.

Muilenburg, James. "Form Criticism and Beyond." *Journal of Biblical Literature* 88 (1969): 1-18

Newsom, Carol A. *The Book of Job : A Contest of Moral Imaginations*. New York: Oxford University Press, 2003.

Niditch, Susan. *War in the Hebrew Bible: A Study in the Ethics of Violence*. New York: Oxford University Press, 1993.

Nolan, Patrick and G. E. Lenski. *Human Societies: An Introduction to Macrosociology*. Eighth edition. New York: McGraw-Hill College, 1999.

Noth, Martin. *The History of Israel*. New York: Harper and Brothers, 1958.

Olmstead, A.A. *A History of the Persian Empire*. Chicago: University of Chicago Press, 1948.

Oeming, Manfred. "'See, We Are Serving Today' (Nehemiah 9:36): Nehemiah as a Theological Interpretation of the Persian Period." Pages 571-88 in *Judah and Judeans in the Persian Period*, edited by Oded Lipschits and Manfred Oeming. Winona Lake, In.: Eisenbrauns, 2006.

Pope, Marvin. *Job*. Anchor Bible. Garden City: Doubleday, 1965.

Porten, Belazel. *The Elephantine Papyri in English: Three Millennia of Cross-Cultural Continuity and Change*. New York: E. J. Brill, 1996.

Porten, Bezalel. "Aramaic Papyri and Parchments: A New Look." *Biblical Archaeologist* 42 (1979): 74-104.

_____. *Archives from Elephantine: The Life of an Ancient Jewish Military Colony*. Berkeley: University of California Press, 1968.

Porten, Bezalel and Ada Yardeni. *Textbook of Aramaic Documents from Ancient Egypt.* 4 vols. Winona Lake, In.: Eisenbrauns, 1986.

Robbins, Vernon K. *Exploring the Texture of Texts: A Guide to Socio-Rhetorical Interpretation.* Valley Forge, Pa: Trinity Press International, 1996.

Sadler Jr., Rodney S. *Can a Cushite Change His Skin? : An Examination of Race, Ethnicity, and Othering in the Hebrew Bible.* JSOTSup 425. New York; London: T&T Clark, 2005.

Saulcy, Felicien Joseph Caignart de. *Étude chronologique des livres d' Esdras et de Néhémie.* Paris: A. Levy, 1868.

Schaeder, H. *Esra der Screiber.* Beiträge zu historischen Theologie 5. Tübingen: J. C. B. Mohr 1930.

Schaper, Joachim. "The Jerusalem Temple as an Instrument of the Achaemenid Fiscal Administration." *Vetus Testamentum* 45, no. 4 (1995): 529-39.

Smith, Daniel L. *The Religion of the Landless : A Social Context of the Babylonian Exile.* Bloomington, In.: Meyer-Stone Books, 1989.

_____. "The Politics of Ezra: Sociological Indicators of Postexilic Judaean Society." in *Second Temple Studies I: Persian Period.* Edited by Philip R. Davies. JSOTSup 117. Sheffield: Sheffield Academic Press, 1991.

Smith, Morton. *Palestinian Parties and Politics that Shaped the Old Testament.* New York: Columbia University Press, 1971.

Smith-Christopher, Daniel L. "Between Ezra and Isaiah: Exclusion, Transformation, and Inclusion of the "Foreigner" in Post-Exilic Biblical Theology." Pages 117-42 in *Ethnicity and the Bible.* Edited by Mark B. Brett. New York: E. J. Brill, 1996.

_____. "The Mixed Marriage Crisis in Ezra 9-10 and Nehemiah 13: A Study of the Sociology of the Post-Exilic Judaean Community." Pages 243-65 in *Second Temple Studies 2: Temple and Community in the Persian Period.* Edited by T. C. Eskenazi and Kent H. Richards. JSOTSup 175. Sheffield: Sheffield Academic Press, 1994.

Southwood, Katherine. "The Holy Seed: The Significance of
    Endogamous Boundaries." Pages 189-224 in *Judah and Judeans
    in the Achaemenid Period*, edited by Oded Lipschits, Gary N.
    Knoppers and Manfred Oeming. Winona Lake, In.: Eisenbrauns,
    2011.

Spiegelberg, W. *Die sogenannte demotische Chronik des Pap. 215 der
    Bibliothèque Nationale du Paris*. Leipzig: 1914.

Stern, E. *The Material Culture of the Land of the Bible in the Persian
    Period (538-332 B.C.E.)*. Warminster: Wilthsire: Aris & Philips;
    Jerusalem: Israel Exploration Society, 1982.

_____. "The Persian Empire and the Political and Social History of
    Palestine in the Persian Period." Vol. 1 of *The Cambridge Histoy
    of Judaism*. Edited by W. D. Davies and L. Finkelstein.
    Cambridge: Cambridge University Press, 1984.

Stolper, Matthew W. *Entrepreneurs and Empire: The Murasu Archive,
    the Murasu Firm, and Persian Rule in Babylonia*, Publications
    de l'Institut et archéologique néerlandais de Stamboul. Leiden,
    Nederland: Nederlands Instituut Voor Het Nabije Oosten, 1985.

_____. "The *šaknu of Nuppur*." *Journal of Cuneiform Studies* 40
    (1988): 127-55.

_____. "Belšunu the Satrap." Pages 389-402 in *Language, Literature
    and History: Philological and Historical Studies Presented to
    Erica Reiner*. Edited by F. Rochberg-Halton. American Oriental
    Series 67. New Haven: American Oriental Society, 1987.

Tavernier, Jan. *Iranica in the Achaemenid Period (ca. 550-330 B.C.):
    Lexicon of Old Iranian Proper Names and Loanwords, Attested
    in Non-Iranian Texts*. Leuven: Peters Publishers and Department
    of Oriental Studies, 2007.

Takekoshi, Yosoburo. *The Economic Aspects of the History of the
    Civilization of Japan*. Vol. 3. New York: Macmillan Press, 1930.

Toorn, K. van der. "Female Prostitution and the Payment of Vows in
    Ancient Israel." *Journal of Biblical Literature* 108 (1989): 193-
    205.

Torrey, C. C. *The Composition and Historical Value of Ezra-Nehemiah*, Beihefte zur Zeitschrift für die alttestamentliche Wissenschaft. Gießen: J. Ricker, 1896.

_____. "The Evolution of a Financier in the Ancient Near East." *Journal of Near Eastern Studies* 2 (1943): 295-301.

_____. *Ezra Studies*. New York: KTAV Publishing House, 1970.

_____. "The Foundry of the Second Temple at Jerusalem." *Journal of Biblical Literature* 55 (1936): 247-60.

Tuplin, Christopher. "Darius' Suez Canal and Persian Imperialism." *Achaemenid History* 6 (1991): 237-83.

Turner, Victor. *From Ritual to Theatre: The Human Seriousness of Play*. New York: Performing Arts Journal Publications, 1982.

Washington, Harold. "The Strange Woman (issah zara/nokriyah) of Proverbs 1-9." Pages 157-85 in *A Feminist Companion to Wisdom Literature*. Edited by Athalya Brenner. Sheffield: Sheffield Academic Press, 1995.

Weinberg, Joel P. *The Citizen-Temple Community*. Translated by Daniel L. Smith-Christopher. JSOTSup 151. Sheffield: Sheffield Academic Press, 1992.

Wellhausen, Julius. *Die Rükkehr der Juden aus dem babylonischen Exil*. Nachrichten von der königlichen Gesellschaft der Wissenschaften zu Göttingen, 1895.

_____. *Prolegomena to the History of Israel*. Translated by J. S. Black and Allan Menzies. 2nd ed. Atlanta: Scholars Press, 1994.

Williamson, H.G.M. *Ezra, Nehemiah*. Waco, Tex.: Word Publishing, 1985.

_____. "Judah and the Jews." Pages 145-63 in *Achaemenid History XI. Studies in Persian History: Essays in Memory of David M. Lewis*. Edited by A. Kuhrt and M. Brosious. Leiden: Nederlands Instituut Voor Het Nabije Oosten, 1998.

Winlock, Herbert Eustis, ed. *The Temple of Hibis in El Khargeh Oasis*. New York: Arno Press, 1941.

Wright, Jacob L. *Rebuilding Identity: The Nehemiah Memoir and Its Earliest Readers*. Berlin: Walter DeGruyter, 2004.

_____. "Surviving in an Imperial Context: Foreign Military Service and Judean Identity." Pages 505-28 in *Judah and Judeans in the Achaemenid Period*, edited by Oded Lipschits, Gary N. Knoppers and Manfred Oeming. 505-28. Winona Lake, In.: Eisenbrauns, 2011.

Wunsch, Cornelia. "Slavery Between Judah and Babylon: The Exilic Experience." Pages 113-134 in *Slaves and Households in the Ancient Near East.* Edited by Laura Culbertson. The Oriental Institute Seminars 7. Chicago: University of Chicago Press, 2011.

Xenophon. *Anabasis.* Translated by Carleton L. Brownson. Loeb Classical Library. Cambridge: Harvard University Press, 2001.

_____. *Cyropaedia.* Translated by Walter Miller. Loeb Classical Library. Cambridge: Harvard University Press, 1994.

Yee, Gale A. *Poor Banished Children of Eve*. Minneapolis: Fortress, 2003.

_____. "Ideological Criticism: Judges 17-21 and the Dismembered Body." Pages 146-70 in *Judges and Method: New Approaches in Biblical Studies*. Edited by Gale A. Yee. Minneapolis: Fortress Press, 1995.

Yoyotte, J. "Les inscriptions hiéroglyphique: Darius et l'Égypt." *Journal Asiatique* 260, no. 3-4 (1972): 253-56.

Zauzich, Karl Theodor. "Die demotischen Papyri von der Insel Elephantine." Pages 421-35 in *Egypt and the Hellenistic World*. Lovanii: Orientaliste, 1983.

www.ingramcontent.com/pod-product-compliance
Lightning Source LLC
Chambersburg PA
CBHW021237090426
42740CB00006B/568